A Concise Guide to Writing a Thesis or Dissertation

A Concise Guide to Writing a Thesis or Dissertation provides clear, succinct, and intentional guidelines about organizing and writing a thesis or dissertation. Part I provides an overview for writing a thesis or dissertation. It describes the big picture of planning and formatting a research study, from identifying a topic to focusing on writing quality. Part II describes the framework and substance of a research study. It models the pattern generally found in a formal, five-chapter research study.

Each chapter of a thesis or dissertation has a specific purpose and this book focuses on each in an easy-to-follow structure. Chapter One reviews the headings and contents expected in the introduction of a study. Chapter Two provides advice for writing a literature review. Chapter Three discusses what to include when describing the methodology. These first three chapters form the proposal section of a study. Two additional chapters present results (Chapter Four) and provide discussion and conclusions (Chapter Five).

Appendices offer resources for instructors and students, including a rubric for evaluating writing, exercises to strengthen skills in APA format, sample purpose statements, a research planning organizer, and a guide for scholarly writing. The book is designed overall to be a practical guide and resource for students for their thesis or dissertation process.

Halyna M. Kornuta provides leadership in faculty professional development, curriculum development, assessment, aligning curriculum with assessment, accreditation and program review. She has been a teacher and an elementary school principal in Canada and Germany, served as vice-president of academic affairs and accreditation liaison officer, and is currently Provost at Reiss-Davis Graduate Center.

Ron W. Germaine has worked in higher education with practicing teachers to guide the design and effect of interventions intended to strengthen their students' learning. He is currently Professor Emeritus, Sanford College of Education, National University, La Jolla, California.

A Concise Guide to Writing a Thesis or Dissertation

Educational Research and Beyond

Second Edition

*Halyna M. Kornuta
and Ron W. Germaine*

Routledge
Taylor & Francis Group

LONDON AND NEW YORK

Second edition published 2019
by Routledge
2 Park Square, Milton Park, Abingdon, Oxon OX14 4RN

and by Routledge
52 Vanderbilt Avenue, New York, NY 10017

Routledge is an imprint of the Taylor & Francis Group, an informa business

First edition self-published 2006

British Library Cataloguing-in-Publication Data
A catalogue record for this book is available from the British Library

Library of Congress Cataloging-in-Publication Data
A catalog record for this book has been requested

ISBN: 978-0-367-17457-6 (hbk)
ISBN: 978-0-367-17458-3 (pbk)
ISBN: 978-0-429-05688-8 (ebk)

Typeset in Galliard
by Apex CoVantage, LLC

What others have said

Over 4000 professors and students have used our book to support the writing of theses or dissertations. Their responses have been overwhelmingly positive, and are captured in the following comments:

Professors

"I recommend your book to my students. It is an excellent, clear guide to structure a thesis or dissertation."

"[Your book] is well written, . . . an easy to read and follow resource that will serve all students who are developing and writing a research project. . . . [It] gives students good advice and examples in addition to great websites for further information . . . It will certainly promote the successful completion of their project. I would recommend this guide to any students who are writing a thesis or a research project of any kind."

"Your book is spot-on for guiding students through writing a thesis. It is short, to the point, and very clear at each step of the way."

"[It] is as clear an explanation as I have seen and will serve students well. We have needed something like this for some time for research classes."

"The book is the most well-organized, concise, and practical guide that I have ever read concerning writing research papers. I intend to use the text in my research writing course as a basic reference tool and required reading for all my students."

And students . . .

"Your Guide helped bring my research project into the realm of the doable." Master's student

"Preparing a research report is a special kind of writing. Your Guide took the mystery out of how to organize what I needed to say." Master's student

"Your book has been the greatest help of any text in my Master's program." Master's student

"I was terrified at the thought of having to write a paper of such magnitude. Your Guide helped me face that fear and find success in writing." Master's student

"I had your book next to me through much of my dissertation because it helped me focus on the purpose of each section . . . you give very easy steps to tackle each part." Doctoral student

"Your book is the best I've read for helping to organize the writing of my dissertation. I am so grateful I have it as a resource." Doctoral student

The authors are grateful to all who have used our book and made valuable suggestions for change.

Need for the second edition

Our first edition modeled fifth edition formatting of the American Psychological Association (APA). This second edition models APA formatting of the sixth edition. Topics, tables, and the evaluation rubric are updated. A research planning organizer and a guide for scholarly writing were added. Some appendices from the first edition have been integrated into the text of the book. We believe the clarity of explanation so many found helpful in the first edition has been maintained. Note to readers: Due to publishing limitations, some of the titles within the book do not accurately conform with APA format. For precise APA format, please see the APA manual (2010, pp. 62–63), or refer to Table 1.1, (p. 8) or Table D.1 (p. 107) in this book.

About the authors

Halyna Kornuta received a B.Ed. in secondary education (mathematics and chemistry), an M.Ed. in educational administration from the University of Saskatchewan, and a doctorate in Leadership Studies from the University of San Diego. Dr. Kornuta has been a P-12 teacher and an elementary school principal in Canada and Germany. She has served in higher education as provost, associate vice president of academic affairs, director of educational effectiveness, and accreditation liaison officer. She has provided leadership and contributed to the literature in faculty professional development, curriculum development, assessment, curriculum alignment with assessment, accreditation, and program review.

Ron Germaine received a BA in geography from the University of British Columbia, an M.Ed. in educational administration from the University of Victoria, and a doctorate in Leadership Studies from the University of San Diego. Dr. Germaine has been a middle school and high school teacher and counselor. His focus in higher education has been with practicing teachers to guide them in designing and measuring the effect of interventions intended to strengthen students' learning. He is currently Professor Emeritus, Sanford College of Education, National University, La Jolla, California. He has published and presented on a variety of topics including program review, accreditation, and twenty-first century skills.

Contents

Part II
Framework and substance of chapters   13

Illustrations

Tables

Figures

Preface

Each journey in educational research is unique. Your completed product will be influenced by many factors including the topic and methodology you choose, your instructors and committee chair, Institutional Review Boards, and the requirements of your institution. It is our hope that you will find this Guide useful, and that it will contribute to making the planning and writing of your study a positive experience while contributing to the quality of your thesis or dissertation.

The purpose of this Guide is to share clear, concise, and intentional practice about organizing and writing a thesis or dissertation. General information about the process is presented in two parts.

Part I provides an overview for writing a thesis or dissertation. It describes the big picture of planning and formatting a research study, from identifying a topic through to writing quality.

Part II describes the framework and substance of a research study. It models the pattern generally found in a formal, five-chapter research study. Each chapter of a research report has a specific purpose. Chapter One reviews the headings and contents expected in an introductory portion of a study. Chapter Two provides advice for writing a literature review. Chapter

Three discusses what to include when describing the methodology for the study. These first three chapters form the proposal section of a study. Two additional chapters present results (Chapter Four), and provide discussion and conclusions (Chapter Five).

The Appendices offer resources for instructors and students, including an evaluation rubric for writing, exercises to strengthen skills in APA format, sample purpose statements, a research planning organizer, and a guide for scholarly writing.

We have enjoyed working with students as they develop their research ideas and writing, and interacting with faculty who have used the Guide. We welcome your comments and suggestions for change. Please email us.

Halyna Kornuta, Ed.D.,
halynakornuta@gmail.com

Ron Germaine, Ed.D.
germaine@nu.edu

The big picture

As you begin the journey of conducting research and reporting the results, it is helpful to know about the formal expectations for writing as well as general organizational guidelines. One set of formal expectations comes from the decision of many of the social and behavioral sciences to follow the American Psychological Association (APA) guidelines for formatting journal articles and research documents. A second set of formal expectations is likely to come from specific requirements set out by your university. Check whether your university has a style guide. Both sets of formal expectations must be adhered to as part of producing quality, professional writing. A third set of expectations may come from your faculty advisor or committee chair about how to structure and develop your study.

Theses and dissertations defined

The term 'thesis' usually refers to a study completed as part of a Master's program, while 'dissertation' refers to the culminating study in a doctoral program. Length and depth of content may also be distinguishing features; however, the purpose of both is to demonstrate that writers have a sufficient knowledge of their field of study. For the purpose of this Guide, reference to a research study (or simply 'a study') includes both a thesis and dissertation, and the general structure for writing a thesis or a dissertation is considered to be the same. Before beginning a study, writers should review institutional requirements for approval of their study. Most studies require approval through an Institutional Review Board (IRB).

Topic development

Begin by identifying a topic about which you feel passionate, and clarify how it fits within your field of study (see Chapter

Two, Figures 2.1 & 2.2). A research study is too much work for its own sake unless you feel some passion for the topic you are investigating. Look within your own professional practice for ideas, discuss ideas with others, including professors, colleagues, and other practitioners. Explaining your interest and answering their questions will help you to focus your ideas, sharpen your purpose, and even lead to a source of support. Choosing a faculty advisor or committee chair that you know you can work with, and one who shares your interests, is critical to the success of your completed study (Lunnenburg & Irby, 2014).

Repeat the discussion process several times as you are articulating the purpose statement, contributing to the Literature Review, and developing the research methodology.

Read the literature within your area of interest, and where possible focus writing assignments from coursework on your topic. You are likely to find several problems or topics that would benefit from an investigation and intervention.

Define the problem clearly.

Articulate the problem or need that must be addressed within the topic you choose. A clearly defined problem will make it much easier to write a laser sharp purpose statement, which will guide the whole of your study. Most problems in social sciences are open-ended questions, and thus do not have "one best solution". For example, there are many kinds of interventions in teaching that may influence students' learning or even their attitudes. The things we want to influence – like measures of achievement or attitude – are dependent variables in a quantitative study. The tools or interventions we use in the process of influencing are independent variables. Clarifying the problem and writing a purpose will be easier when you define a problem in terms of: What effect does [some intervention or strategy] have on [measures of what you want to influence]?

For example, a problem might be: How do cooperative learning/teaching strategies affect the academic achievement of learners in an elementary school setting? Or: What effect does teaching a multicultural-based curriculum have on adolescent learners' attitudes towards tolerance? Or: What effect does parent involvement in the life of a school have on the graduation rate of children? A significant body of educational research has been performed around such questions and is readily available in the literature. Reading the current literature begins to define a topic for further investigation.

Choose the methodology.

Consider what you might measure, who you would interview or survey, or what documents you might examine to gather data about the problem you have identified. For example, measures of whether a teaching intervention is successful could come from sources such as test scores, office referrals, attendance, et cetera. Such numerical measures are called *quantitative* data. You may also discover what you need to learn by interviewing people who have experienced what you are investigating. Such verbal or written data are called *qualitative* data.

Craft a purpose statement.

Once the problem is defined and the methodology identified, a purpose statement is needed. The purpose statement is a clear, precise statement that encapsulates what you intend to do in your study. The purpose statement is like a 'rudder' that guides everything you write in your study. Each time the purpose statement is repeated in your study, it should be copied and pasted so that it is exactly the same. Part II, Chapter One provides more detailed information about writing the purpose statement.

Organization

Writing a research study should demonstrate understanding of how to prepare for, set up, and conduct quality research. In general, this requires identifying a topic, finding out and reporting from the literature what is already known about the topic, what other researchers have discovered, establishing a need and purpose for the study, detailing a plan for gathering and analyzing data, results, and making recommendations.

Chapters One, Two and Three.

On the surface, the logical order for writing a research study may appear to begin with Chapter One and proceed sequentially through to Chapter Five.

> *The order for writing a research study begins with Chapter Two, followed by Chapters One, Three, Four, and Five.*

However, because research must be grounded in literature, the place to begin is with the Chapter Two review of literature, followed by Chapter One, which introduces the study; then Chapter Three, which presents the plan for gathering and analyzing data, followed by Chapter Four with its presentation and analysis of data, and finally the executive summary of Chapter Five, which discusses the findings, draws conclusions, and looks ahead to make recommendations for change in policy or practice and need for further study.

Suggestions for choosing a topic and beginning the Literature Review are found in Part II, Chapter Two of this Guide. The Literature Review for your area of focus should reflect current knowledge about the topic to be investigated, and should review what other researchers have discovered about the issue, or closely related topics. It is important to write about the topic with sufficient breadth to present differing perspectives or contrasting views of the topic, and with sufficient depth to report the complexities of the issue.

Upon completion of Chapter Two, Chapter One is written. It outlines the need, purpose, and nature of the study. Chapter Three is written after Chapter One is completed and describes the methodology for carrying out the study. Completion of the first three chapters ends the proposal-writing stage. If you have not already done so, check with your advisor about requirements for approval from your institution's IRB before beginning data collection.

Chapters Four and Five.
Once the proposal is approved by an IRB, data are gathered and analyzed. Two additional chapters are then added to the three-chapter proposal section. Chapter Four presents the findings and analysis of data. Chapter Five forms an executive summary of the study and includes recommendations for change in policy or practice, and recommendations for further study. Each of the five chapters should be 'stand alone'; written so that the reader could read one chapter and know the essence of the study.

References and Abstract.
The reference section begins on a new page at the end of your writing, and before any appendices. We highly recommend keeping an ongoing, annotated bibliography throughout the writing process as a way of tracking key ideas and sources. Notes and ideas from each source are briefly summarized within an annotated bibliography, and the source identified in APA format so

that it is available for the reference section. The annotated bibliography will provide a quick link for you to go back to sources, which is often needed during writing. An example of an entry in an annotated bibliography is:

> Marshall, J., Smart, J., & Alston, D. (2016). Development and validation of Teacher Intentionality of Practice Scale (TIPS): A measure to evaluate and scaffold professional development. *Teaching and Teacher Education, 59,* 159–168. doi:10.1016/j.tate.2016.05.007
>
> The Marshall et al. article identifies seven teacher-controllable actions that are said to lead to greater student success. Note to self: Compare/align the seven actions with other measures of teacher effectiveness to see how they match.

In the reference section of your report, list only the references you actually cite in your writing, and omit all notes from the annotated bibliography.

The Abstract should be the very last part of your writing. Information about writing an abstract is at the beginning of Part II of this Guide, and in the APA Publication Manual (APA, 2010b, pp. 25–27).

Writing quality

Writing should reflect grammatical correctness, clear and precise communication, accuracy of information, and a logical flow of thought. Chapters Three and Four of the *Publication Manual of the American Psychological Association* (APA, 2010b) provide excellent advice about writing style. The APA Publication Manual also identifies a format for levels of headings. Headings are 'directional signs' within your writing. They help to create meaning for readers by showing a pattern of organization and flow of thought; therefore, accurate formatting of headings is essential. Critical thinking contributes to clarity in writing.

Levels of headings.

Headings show readers the outline and flow of thought for your writing. In that sense, headings are like navigation lights mariners rely on as they traverse a dark channel at night. Without the navigation lights, sailors would quickly become lost or run aground. Similarly, without correct levels of headings that reflect accurate formatting, readers will have difficulty following what you are trying to communicate. Therefore, it is essential to use the format for headings shown in Table I.1 below (APA, 2010b, pp. 62–63). You may not need all of the levels, but it is essential that you follow the pattern to the extent necessary for your specific study.

Table I.1

Format for APA levels of headings

Format for five levels of headings	
Level of heading	*Format*
1	**Centered, Boldface, Uppercase and Lowercase Heading**
2	**Flush Left, Boldface, Uppercase and Lowercase Heading**
3	**Indented, boldface, lowercase paragraph heading ending with a period.**
4	***Indented, boldface, italicized, lowercase paragraph heading ending with a period.***
5	*Indented, italicized, lowercase paragraph heading ending with a period.*

Additional strategies to enhance quality writing include repeating the purpose statement word for word in each place it is stated so that its precise focus is not lost or changed. Key words should be used consistently. For example, a term such as 'educational workshops' should not reappear as 'educational in-service sessions.' A research study should not be written from the bias of one particular perspective. Fairmindedness and intellectual integrity require that contrasting views or differing perspectives be presented.

Table of Contents.
It is possible to create a Table of Contents by using a formatting function in Microsoft Word (web search 'Creating a Table of Contents in MS Word'). Formatting the headings in this way will allow you to create a Table of Contents that digitally links each heading in your study to a page location.

Format.
The APA Publication Manual (APA, 2010b) was written primarily as a guide for writing manuscripts for journals. While most of the APA formatting requirements apply to research papers, theses, or dissertations, some differences in style are both permissible and encouraged. "The Publication Manual presents explicit style requirements but acknowledges that alternatives are sometimes necessary; authors should balance the rules of the Publication Manual with good judgment" (APA, 2010b, p. 5). It is also important to check formatting requirements unique to your own institution. In general, the preference is for 12-point font with a typeface such as Times New Roman. Double-space all text lines, and singe-space the text in tables and figures.

Requirements for margin size may vary. If the final product is to be bound, be sure to check with your university about the appropriate margin size. If the final product is not bound, all margins should be one inch (APA, 2010b). An exception is the first page of each chapter, which should begin with a two-inch margin (rather than one inch) at the top of the page. Additional specific requirements can be found in the APA Publication Manual, section 8.03.

All pages must be numbered consecutively beginning with the Title Page as page one. Page numbers are located in the top right of the header. Also in the header, flush left, should be the running head, an abbreviated form of the title that is no longer than 50 characters.

Writing resources

The *Publication Manual of the American Psychological Association* (APA, 2010b) is an excellent resource for guiding scholarly writing in terms of style, mechanics, and formatting. A helpful online resource is available at http://www.apastyle.org/learn/faqs/index.aspx

Other helpful resources include a page on the University of Toronto website, http://www.writing.utoronto.ca/advice/specific-types-of-writing/literature-review, for advice about writing a literature review. Additionally, the webpage, http://www.writing.utoronto.ca/advice/style-and-editing/hit-parade-of-errors, provides examples of what to do and what not to do in relation to writing style, grammar, and punctuation.

Tables and figures.
Tables and figures have unique formatting elements as defined by the APA Publication Manual (APA, 2010b). Tables are usually used for information to be displayed in rows and columns. The title for a table is placed above the table in two lines: The first line states the table number, in plain text, and not followed by a period. The second line states the table name, in italics and

capital letters for each word in the title. A formatting example for tables follows.

Table 1
Alignment of *Outcomes, Assessments, and Assignments*

Figures are usually diagrams and illustrations. Only one line is used to state the figure number, in italics, and the figure name. This line is placed under the figure. The figure name is not in italics and only the first word is capitalized. A formatting example for figures follows.

Figure 1. Relationships to program learning outcomes

All tables and figures must be referred to in the main body of the text and in the order in which they appear.

Process and product

A significant time commitment is required to complete a research proposal, and to carry out the study. Students have estimated that the process of developing and prioritizing ideas requires a minimum of 30 hours, the Literature Review 80 hours, and the methodological framework 30 hours. The initial stages of writing often include a feeling of uncertainty. This 'muddling through' stage is typical as your ideas develop and evolve. Chapter Two of this Guide provides advice on identifying and developing a topic for a study.

In the research phase, time for data gathering can range from days to several months or years, depending on the nature and purpose of the study. To help view your writing from the perspective of someone who will evaluate it, an example of a grading rubric is included in the appendices. The rubric provides descriptions of categories and levels of quality for research writing.

The total number of pages for a research study may range from fewer than 100 to more than 300, including Title Page, Abstract, Table of Contents, and References. Far more important than the number of pages, however, is that the content reflects scholarship and clear logic, and provides accurate, fair-minded communication that has a logical flow of thought. When this type of writing is combined with a passion for the topic, an excellent product is likely to result.

Summary

Part I of the Guide has presented a big picture view of the contents of a research study, along with the general formatting requirements. Part II will describe the focus and contents of each chapter.

Framework and substance of chapters

Part II of the Guide offers a pattern for preparing and reporting a formal research study. However, it is important to note that individual institutions are unique and have their own specific requirements, and therefore the pattern provided in this book may need to be adapted.

This Guide describes the contents of each chapter in a formal research study. The following pages are arranged and sequenced to model the appropriate format. Each of the five chapters in Part II provides examples of topics that should be addressed and headings to be used. Chapter One reviews the requirements for introducing the study. Chapter Two provides suggestions for the process of finding, selecting, and developing the topic through a Literature Review. Ideas for organizing time and information are also presented. Chapter Three discusses what to include when describing the methodology for the study. Chapter Four provides a model for presenting data gathered and for analyzing the information, while Chapter Five provides suggestions for concluding the study.

Introductory pages

Part II begins with an example of a Title Page and other introductory pages that may be included.

Title Page.

Title

Submitted to
[Instructor's Name]

By
[Your Name]

In partial fulfillment of the requirements for
[Indicate the degree or course]

[Your University]

[M/D/Y]

Additional pages.

Dissertations and some theses will need the additional pages shown below. Be sure to check with your faculty advisor about the requirements and format at your institution.

Page for Certification of Approval

Page for Signatures of Advisors and dates

Page for Dedication and Acknowledgements

A Dedication and Acknowledgements page is optional. This personal section is guided by the individuality of the writer. You are invited to dedicate your writing and acknowledge people who have contributed to your development, who have special meaning to you, or who have helped make the task of writing possible.

Abstract.

The purpose of an Abstract is to provide readers with a concise and accurate overview of the study in a maximum of 350 words. The Abstract states the purpose, research questions, methodology, description of participants (or subjects), as well as how the participants were or will be involved in the study. While the Abstract appears prior to Chapter One, it is written after you have completed all of the chapters so that an accurate summary is possible.

Assistance for writing an Abstract can be found in the *APA Publication Manual* (APA, 2010b), pages 25 to 27. Note that the word count for the Abstract referred to in the APA Manual is for journal articles, not theses or dissertations. Another source for assistance in writing the Abstract is at *http://www.writing. utoronto.ca/advice/specific-types-of-writing/abstract.*

The remainder of Part II includes specifics about the structure and substance of each of the five chapters.

Introduction

Chapter One of a research study introduces the study. Chapter One and each subsequent chapter begins with an untitled introductory section that indicates what is to follow. Immediately after the introductory section is the body of the chapter, which is typically divided by headings. The chapter concludes with a summary that reviews what was said in the chapter and also includes a bridge to the following chapter. Chapter One of this Guide will describe the sections that should be included in your first chapter and will provide examples of what key statements might look like. Most of the first three chapters of a dissertation or thesis are written in future tense. When the proposal section is approved and the study carried out, Chapters One, Two, and Three are re-written in past tense. As noted in Part I, Chapter One is generally written after the Chapter Two Literature Review is completed.

Chapter One of a research study is an overview of the whole study. When writing this chapter:

- Use appropriate APA style for page numbers, headings, and citing authors;
- Use future tense to describe what you plan to do in your study;

- Use past tense when describing what others have found at a specific time in the past (APA, 2010b), for example "Anderson (2017) reported . . ." or "Daniels (2017) stated . . .;
- Avoid value statements (should, needs to, must . . .);
- Use citations from the literature to support what you say. Direct quotes should be used sparingly, and should be introduced so that they flow smoothly into your writing;
- During your writing, continue with an annotated bibliography which should be started as part of the Literature Review (see Chapter Two, pp. 35 and 40). The annotated bibliography is not a formal part of the research study but will be helpful throughout your writing and in composing the reference section.

A reference section is required to represent the whole of your writing. All references must be in APA format. References should:

- Be current – within the last ten years – though exceptions are necessary for 'foundation' authors. For example, writers in education might include foundational authors such as Dewey (1916); Piaget (1954); or Burns (1978);
- Provide reference to authors who present contrasting points of view; and
- Include more primary sources than secondary sources:
  - o *Primary sources:* Journal articles, books, papers presented at conferences, specialized indexes, bibliographies, abstracts, and reviews of research. They are reports of experts' own research, and thus are like eyewitness accounts of completed studies.
  - o *Secondary sources:* These sources do not provide firsthand or eyewitness accounts. They are compilations, analyses, and interpretation of primary sources of information.

Electronic communications, such as email, are not cited because they are not retrievable. If used, they are cited in the body of the text only. Include only references of books or documents you have read.

A full research study is likely to reference 30 or more sources. However, rather than count the number of references, the real goal is to have readers say, "This person understands the topic well because s/he has thoroughly reported evidence about the depth and breadth of the topic; and the writing reflects the purpose statement." The writing should provide a strong theoretical support that shows what other experts have found and reported in the area you are proposing to investigate.

Headings

This section identifies and discusses ten headings that could appear in Chapter One. The discussion provides guidelines for what should be included in your proposal. Note that the particular format for your headings should follow APA levels of headings (APA, 2010b, p. 62; this Guide, Table I.1).

Chapter One begins with an untitled introductory section that may be from one to several paragraphs in length. This introductory section will not have a heading. The purpose of the introductory section is to set the stage for the study by identifying the general problem to be investigated and communicating information essential to what will follow in the chapter. The introduction does not include technical detail. It is an orientation section that starts with a general statement and proceeds to focus on a specific problem. For example, mathematics teacher Linda VanSolkema wrote the following introductory section in Chapter One of a study she carried out about how girls' confidence in mathematics is formed:

One of the purposes of education is to provide the tools necessary for the development of an analytical mind (King,

1948; Bloom, 1956). King stated, "The function of education is to teach one to think intensively and to think critically" (King, p. 48). One of the ways to prepare students for rigor of thought is to work with them in mathematics to develop maturity in logic and reasoning.

Each person is unique and has aptitudes for different fields of study. Society often sees each gender with its own field of specialty: women excelling at language arts and men in math and science. Women are not usually expected to excel at math. Educators may need to overcome the stereotypical gender differences imposed on women to help prepare women for mathematical rigor.

One of the most prominently mentioned affective variables in determining math ability is confidence. Confidence in one's ability to do math significantly differentiates the genders. Boys are more likely to overrate their abilities and have high confidence, while girls commonly underrate their abilities and have low confidence in their math abilities (Green, DeBacker, Ravindran & Krows, 1999). While studies have shown the variation of confidence between the genders, there is a need to explore how this confidence is formed and how teachers might intervene to help build high confidence for all students.

Chapter One will present an overview of the study by introducing the background and purpose of the study, the significance of the study, and the limitations and delimitations of the study.

(VanSolkema, 2003)

Chapter One of VanSolkema's study then introduced each section in the remainder of the chapter with a heading. The headings followed the same order as those listed in the last sentence of her introduction.

Background to the study.

The background presents the 'big picture,' identifying the context of the problem to be investigated. It sets the stage for the relevance and purpose of the study. This section contains a history of the issue you are investigating and how it was dealt with in the past.

The background provides a discussion of how the problem developed over time, trends related to the issue, and unresolved elements and/or social concerns. For example, when addressing the background of how the needs of students with disabilities have been handled in the past, you might write about how they have been segregated, provided with Individualized Education Plans, and mainstreamed. Pertinent elements of legislation are also likely to be relevant here.

> *For years, there has been a concern about the colors of M&M's® and whether they are represented equally in a box of M&M's® (Author, Year).*

Cite recognized authors/researchers to let the reader be aware that you are not just expressing your own ideas, and to support and strengthen the statements you are making. A search of resources is essential to know who and what to quote.

The background serves to underscore why your study should be done in the context of previous studies. It uncovers a problem or issue where further research is required. It expands on the statement, "While studies have shown . . . there is a need to . . ." The background section – and more broadly, the whole of your study – is guided by the purpose of your study, identifying what you, the researcher, hope to discover.

Purpose of the study.

A research study should not be undertaken to prove a point; it must reflect integrity and report candidly even when the results turn out to be different than what you had hoped. Your study should stand up to the scrutiny of differing opinions because of the veracity of methodology and reporting. When bias is shown, arguments are likely to convince only those who are already persuaded to your perspective.

Qualitative example: The purpose of this qualitative study is to describe the perceptions and expectations of M&M consumers about the colors and quantities of candies in a box of M&M's®.

Quantitative example: The purpose of this quantitative study is to determine the numerical relationship between the colors of candies in a box of M&M's®.

All phases of the study, from careful research design through reporting of results, should reflect fairmindedness and integrity.

Guiding questions for preparing a purpose statement.

Writing a purpose statement requires articulating a problem, which can be clarified through a series of questions that flow from general to specific (see Part I, Define the problem clearly).

1. What topic requiring investigation am I passionate about? It is important to choose an area of focus that is personally motivating. A study should not be undertaken simply to prove a point, but rather to investigate and look for evidence that will stand up to critical review.

2. What is a problem in your area of interest that would help or strengthen your professional practice if answers could be found?
3. Who is likely to benefit if the problem you describe were resolved?
4. What would you measure, or to whom would you talk, to gather data needed for your investigation?

A well-written purpose statement avoids bias, and is a critical component to the success of any research proposal. It establishes the direction for the research, much like the rails establish direction for a train. Work hard at making the purpose clear and precise. Capture the essence of the study in a single sentence, or at most, two sentences. Communicate your purpose statement with others, and listen to their questions and feedback. Ary, Jacobs, Razavieh, and Sorensen (2006) pointed out that when the researcher is able to articulate a clear, precise purpose statement, s/he has accomplished one of the most difficult phases of the research process.

The purpose statement will appear in all five chapters. To ensure the integrity of the purpose throughout the whole of the document, we strongly recommend copying and pasting the purpose statement each time it is used.

The Purpose of the Study section should be short. It presents a precise and effective way to deal with the problem already identified. In some studies, this section may be titled, Statement of the Problem. It is essential that the purpose statement be written as clearly, as precisely, and as concisely as possible. The purpose statement should be goal oriented, emphasize the outcomes, and state the research methodology you will use. Certain words particular to the methodology should be used as shown in Table 1.1.

A qualitative purpose statement might say, "The purpose of this qualitative study is to *discover*, through the perceptions and

Table 1.1

Words particular to a methodology

Qualitative Terminology	Quantitative Terminology
Describe	Determine
Develop	Compare
Discover	Investigate
Explore	Test

experiences of teachers who work with peer tutoring programs, the advantages and disadvantages of such programs and key strategies for developing and maintaining the programs."

A quantitative purpose statement might say, "The purpose of this quantitative study is to *determine* the relationship between measures of success of two sex education programs and similar measures of student sexual activity in a school district in Southern California."

The purpose statement *must* be consistent when repeated in each chapter. We advise copying and pasting the purpose statement in each place it is used. If a purpose statement is not clear and precise in the writer's mind, it is likely to be written in different ways in different places within the writing. The following statements illustrate the inconsistency of a purpose statement dawn from different places in an early draft of a proposal:

- The focus of this study is to address gender bias in the classroom and *to show* that teaching practices influence learning in students.
- The focus of this study is to determine if gender bias exists in our classrooms through the current literature in the reading curriculum and the lack of positive or nontraditional role models that are offered to them.
- This research proposal will investigate the problem of gender bias and the effect of academic success of female students, and why it continues to be an issue in today's classrooms.

- This proposal will investigate how practitioners' perception of gender bias is shown through the literature used to teach children to read, through teacher-student interaction, and through the emphasis on male achievement in mathematics, science, and technology classes.

When the writer became aware of the wide range of purpose statements, she re-examined her purpose, and wrote a statement that more precisely captured her intent. She consistently used the following throughout each chapter:

The purpose of this qualitative study is to describe the feelings, perceptions, and practices of teachers who are knowledgeable about Title IX and who implement the spirit of gender equality in their classrooms.

Personal statement.
Including a personal statement is optional. If it is included in Chapter One, it is a sub-section of the purpose section. It may be important to write a personal statement if you feel particularly passionate about the topic you want to research. The research itself must be conducted without bias and must be seen by others to be conducted without bias; however, the reality is that we each bring our own perspectives to what we observe. It is better to be upfront with bias rather than to try to hide it. Personal awareness of bias is an important step in setting bias aside as you carry out a study and report the results. If a personal statement is included in Chapter One, it is written in the first person. It is a brief section about the writer's interest in the problem and may begin, "The motivation for this study came from my . . ."

Research question.
The purpose statement is the primary guide for all phases of the study, from the literature through the methodology, data analysis, and recommendations. Not surprisingly, the purpose

statement forms the basis of the research question. A simple way to create a research question that parallels the purpose statement is to turn the purpose statement into a question.

Qualitative example: What are the perceptions and expectations of M&M® consumers about the colors and quantities of candies in a box of M&M's®?

Quantitative example: What is the numerical relationship between the number of each color of candies in a box of M&M's® and the total number of candies?

A statement such as: "The purpose of this quantitative study is to determine the relationship between measures of [. . .] and [. . .]" is turned into a research question by asking: "What is the relationship between measures of [. . .] and [. . .]?" Avoid using research questions that have a "yes" or "no" answer.

Typically, one or two questions are formed from one purpose statement, but there may be more. Be sure to provide an introduction to the questions. Possible introductions are:

- "Based on the purpose of this study, the two research questions are . . ."
- "The following research questions will guide the Literature Review and Methodology of this Research Study: . . ."
- "The following research questions will guide data collection: . . ."
- "This quantitative study will focus on answering the following questions . . ."

Examples of writing research questions.

Given the purpose statement, "The purpose of this qualitative study is to describe the feelings, perceptions, and practices of

teachers who are knowledgeable about Title IX and who implement the spirit of gender equality in their classrooms," two
research questions are likely:

1. What does the spirit of gender equality look like when
   teachers live it out in their classrooms?
2. What are the feelings, perceptions, and practices of teachers
   who are knowledgeable to Title IX and who implement the
   spirit of gender equality in their classrooms?

One further example is presented to illustrate how clarity and
precision are needed in developing a research question. For the
purpose statement, "The purpose of this quantitative study is to
determine the relationship between measures of success in school
of similar groups of middle school students: groups that are tracked
according to ability, groups that are not tracked," the researcher's
task is clear: Identify the tracks; identify valid and reliable measures
of student success; gather data; and analyze and compare data for
similar groups – those that are tracked with those that are not.

An imprecise research question might ask: "How does ability
grouping of students for instruction at the middle school effect
individual students' measures of success at school?" Notice that
the researcher could pursue a variety of paths to try to answer
the question: He may compare measures of success; talk to students and ask them about their perceptions; talk to teachers to
ask them about what they think; or talk to other groups, such as
parents, to find out their experience. The question is therefore
too broad in nature and gives no clear indication about how it
might be answered or accomplished.

A much clearer, precise research question would be: "What is
the statistical relationship between measures of success in school
of similar groups of middle school students: groups that are
tracked according to ability, groups that are not tracked?" The
question clearly aligns with the purpose statement by turning
the purpose statement directly into a question.

Significance of the study.

The Significance of the Study describes the importance, or the 'so what?' of the study. It makes clear why the research is important and to whom it is important. In this section:

- Elaborate on how the research will be of importance and how it will help improve practice. Who will it help and how? Will it provide a stepping-stone for others to go further?
- What benefits would occur if definitive answers were found to the research question?
- If you find a gap in the literature about the topic, describe the contribution the study will make.

> *Knowledge of the perceptions and expectations of M&M's®* *consumers about the colors and quantities of candies in a* *box of M&M's® will contribute to improved product devel-* *opment and increased customer satisfaction.*

The following is an example from the significance of a study that investigated the use of communication technologies to improve interpersonal relationships of emotionally disturbed students.

> Findings from the study will reveal insights from teachers who used technology in working with emotionally disturbed students. Thus, the study will contribute to special educators' knowledge about the use of technology to promote growth in the social and emotional life of emotionally disturbed students. The findings may have implications for the students, their parents, and the funding policy for technology within the school district. In addition, while the focus of this study is a special day class for emotionally

disturbed students at the elementary school level, the study could be replicated for students of varying disabilities and grade levels. The study may therefore have significance for teacher-researchers at other grade levels.

(McGowan, 2003)

Assumptions.
Assumptions must be identified for a study that employs quantitative methodologies only. No assumptions are made prior to starting qualitative studies because such studies begin with a search for an understanding of the whole, and any assumptions prior to the start of qualitative studies may distort the findings.

> *Assumption: The sample size is representative of the greater population of M&M's® boxes.*

For quantitative studies, an assumption is any important 'fact' that is presumed to be true but not verifiable. For example, assumptions important to the carrying out of a study may include items such as:

- The participants in this study will answer survey questions honestly.
- The treatment was administered in the same way in different classrooms.
- The scores of other students do not influence an individual student's score on the same measure.
- The pre-test and post-test were administered in the same way and under the same conditions.

Assumptions are to be written in paragraph format.

Limitations.

Limitations identify potential weaknesses of the study from sources that are outside of the control of the researcher. Limitations are restrictions on the extent or type of data that are available. Limitations may also restrict the generalizability of findings.

> Limitation: *Available samples of M&M's® are limited to those packed by the company during the six-month period prior to the start of the study.*

For example, if the population from whom you gather data is 80 percent Hispanic, the findings may not be generalizable to other populations made up of a lesser percentage Hispanics. The fact that a study has limitations does not mean it is a weak study. However, it is important for researchers to communicate awareness of limitations by directly addressing them in Chapter One. Some examples of limitations are:

- The number of people who could be involved;
- The number of people who could be interviewed in a finite amount of time;
- The number of schools available;
- The subjects who completed . . . in the last five years;
- For this study, of 6000 potential subjects, 5994 threw away their records leaving only six available to participate. The fact that only six subjects can be included is a limitation to the study because it is something outside the control of the researcher.

Limitations are to be written in paragraph format. Being upfront with limitations and delimitations adds credibility to a study, as noted in the following section.

Delimitations.

Delimitations address how the study will be narrowed in scope by the researcher. Delimitations form boundaries that the researcher chooses so that the study is more focused or manageable. Such boundaries are often needed; however, the researcher must recognize the implications of the delimitations on the generalizability of findings of the study. Some examples of delimitations are:

- The uniqueness of the setting, for example "The study will be confined to interviewing and observing at one school that has specific demographic characteristics."
- The nature and size of the sample, for example "For this research, six schools will be chosen to be part of the study." (rather than trying to include a much larger number of schools that might be available)
- "This study describes the influence of the program through the eyes of five high school students." Note that in this latter example, the researcher has chosen not to interview teachers, administrators, or a greater number of students.

> Delimitation: *For the purposes of this study, the researcher chose boxes of M&M's® from 12 store locations in Southern California.*

Delimitations are to be written in paragraph format.

Definitions.

Define words that have special meaning for your study or words that may be unclear. Consider the audience who may read your study, and include terminology that will assist in their understanding. This section could be introduced with a statement such as: "The following terms are defined to clarify their meaning and use in the study." Consider defining:

- Key terms. For example, "Reader's Workshop is . . ." or "Social and emotional learning (SEL) is defined in this study as . . ."
- Terms specific to their use in the study. For example, "Group membership refers to whether a student was in the treatment group or in the control group."
- Words that may be vague or open to misinterpretation, or words that may be new to the reader. Assume the reader does not have the contextual understanding of your study. For example, "In this study, success in school refers to a variable created by averaging two measures: academic achievement and behavior."

Write the definitions in complete sentences. If the heading, Definitions, is a level two heading, the word or term to be defined should be a level three heading as shown below.

M&M's®.
M&M's® are small candy-coated chocolates of various colors.
M&M's® Box.
M&M's® are packaged to contain approximately 50 candies per box.

Summary.
In this final section of Chapter One, provide a succinct summary of what you have written in the chapter.

To add to the clarity of your writing, say what you are going to say; say it; then say what you said.

The introductory part of each chapter tells what you are going to say; the body of the chapter says what you want to say; and the summary of the chapter says briefly what you have said. Each chapter summary should end with a brief introduction of what is to come in the next chapter.

Chapter summary

In this Guide, Chapter One has identified and discussed headings that could appear in Chapter One of your study. Chapter Two will introduce the important issues of identifying a topic and beginning the Literature Review, and will then introduce two main sub-headings that most topics will require.

For further information on the topics addressed in the preceding chapter, see Ary et al. (2006); M. Gall, J. Gall, and Borg (2006); Mertens (2015); Trochim and Donnelly (2007).

Review of the literature

Chapter Two of this Guide presents advice on identifying and developing a topic for a research study, and discusses the specific elements that make up the Literature Review of Chapter Two of the study.

Recall that the purpose of this Guide is to provide direction for those who are writing a research study, whether it be a research proposal, a thesis, or a dissertation. Part of the preparation for any study is a Literature Review. The purpose of a Literature Review is to provide readers with a context for the study in terms of the historical background of the issue, the theoretical framework for the topic, and different perspectives, and to report on studies of a similar nature. Note that the Literature Review is *not* the research itself but helps set the context for the study and points to the significance of the research you plan to do.

A good Literature Review summarizes and critiques related studies and shows how their findings link to the problem being investigated. A good Literature Review should also present contrasting views about the topic. As Noll (2011) stated, "Controversy prompts reexamination and perhaps renewal" (p. v). It is important to communicate to readers that differing perspectives on the topic are being considered, and that a valid basis exists for further study. (Authors' note: The *Taking Sides* series from McGraw-Hill is an excellent source of contrasting views about many topics in education. For further information, see "Noll" in the reference section.)

The review of the literature provides an important connection between existing knowledge and the problem being investigated. It sets the issue you will study in the context of a bigger picture. In so doing, the information provided in the Literature Review moves from the general to the specific and from older perspectives of the topic to more recent perspectives. As your Literature Review becomes more focused, you may find your purpose statement needs refining (Springer, 2010).

It is pertinent to mention what a Literature Review is not. It is not primarily a collection of quotations from other writers. While reporting about the findings and perspectives of others is an important part of the Literature Review, it must be done in a way in which your own flow of thought and organization is evident. Paraphrasing ideas, and comparing and contrasting perspectives expressed by different writers are important considerations in constructing the Literature Review. Avoid plagiarism by giving credit when paraphrasing or quoting someone else's ideas or words.

When writing a thesis or dissertation, students should ideally engage in choosing a research topic near the beginning of a program. Throughout other course work, items related to the topic may be discussed with others, and summaries of reading can be added to an annotated bibliography. Experience, interaction with others, and reading literature in your area of interest will contribute to a clearer development of your topic and purpose, and ease the burden of the overall task (Ary et al., 2010).

Brainstorming and organizing content for the Literature Review

Plot your area of interest and topics that link to it. Use an organizing structure, such as a fishbone diagram, concept map, or an outline to organize your thoughts. The fishbone diagram shown in Figure 2.1 is an example of an organizer used in a Literature

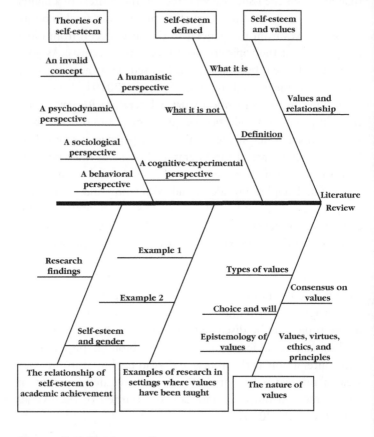

Figure 2.1 Fishbone diagram

Review for a study on the relationship of self-esteem and values. Note how the topics transfer to headings for a Literature Review. A concept map is another form of an organizer, shown in Figure 2.2, as used in a Literature Review for a study on the use of portfolios in the developmental supervision of teachers.

The topics in the fishbone organizer would look like the following when formatted in APA headings in a Literature Review.

Theories of Self-Esteem
Self-esteem as an invalid concept.
Self-esteem from a psychodynamic perspective.
Self-esteem from a sociological perspective.
Self-esteem from a behavior perspective.

Self-Esteem Defined
What self-esteem is.
What self-esteem is not.
Definition.

Self-Esteem and Values
Values and relationships.

The Relationship of Self-Esteem to Academic Achievement
Research findings.
Gender-specific issues.

Examples of Research in Settings Where Values Have Been Taught
Example 1.
Example 2.

The Nature of Values
Values, virtues, ethics, and principles.
Epistemology of values.
Types of values.
Choice and will.
Consensus on values.

The concept map in Figure 2.2 is another example of an organizer. In this case, it shows the organization of a Literature Review for a study on the use of portfolios in the developmental supervision of teachers.

The topics in the concept map would look like the following when formatted as APA headings.

Professional Development
    Adult stages of development.
        Generativity vs. stagnation.
        Career stages.

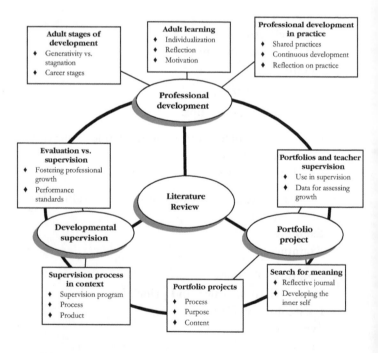

Figure 2.2 Concept map

Adult learning.
>   *Individualization.*
>   *Reflection.*
>   *Motivation.*

Professional development in practice.
>   *Shared practices.*
>   *Continuous development.*
>   *Reflection on practice.*

Developmental Supervision
Evaluation vs. supervision.
>   *Fostering professional growth.*
>   *Performance standards.*

Supervision process in context.
>   *Supervision program.*
>   *Process.*
>   *Product.*

Portfolio Project
Portfolios and teacher supervision.
>   *Use in supervision.*
>   *Data for assessing growth.*

Search for meaning.
>   *Reflective journal.*
>   *Developing the inner self.*

Portfolio projects.
>   *Process.*
>   *Purpose.*
>   *Content.*

Beginning the Literature Review

The following suggestions, individually or in combination, may be helpful in beginning the Literature Review. The suggestions are noted as a checklist that may be used as you develop your own system.

☐ Maintain an ongoing annotated bibliography for all of the journal articles, books, and web sources you read. A one or two sentence summary provides a quick reminder of the information, or you may expand to include ideas or perspectives that will be helpful to your Literature Review. Add the source in APA format so that all information is available for the reference section. For example:

> Paul, R., & Elder, L. (2014). *The miniature guide to critical thinking concepts and tools.* Tomales, CA: Foundation for Critical Thinking.
>
> . . . a concise articulation of the principles of critical thinking in ways that are applicable to all content areas. The concept of intellectual virtues thinking links critical thinking to constructive communication and principles required for civic discourse.
>
> When each source is made part of an annotated bibliography, much time is saved when it comes time to creating a reference section because all sources are already within one document. An example of an annotated bibliography is available at http://www.writing.utoronto.ca/advice/specific-types-of-writing/annotated-bibliography

☐ Use assignments from classes to begin building a review of the literature related to your topics of interest.

☐ Develop a systematic topic identification procedure. For print sources, use colored tabs in journals or books sections to locate relevant information. Bookmark online sources in one or more specific folders.

☐ Begin an Idea Notebook. Include titles of books, journal articles, websites, and ideas that can be developed at another time. These will be resources for your area of interest.

☐ Search electronic databases. Most libraries offer instruction in the skills needed for searching.

☐ When reading the conclusions of studies, note the unanswered questions and comments about the 'need for further study.' Such questions and comments might provide direction for your study.

☐ Use the references in articles to find additional resources.

☐ Become knowledgeable about particular research methodologies. Qualitative and quantitative methodology and Action Research are discussed in Chapter Three of this Guide.

☐ Read completed research reports, theses, or dissertations.

☐ Begin thinking about a title for your study. The title should be brief (no more than 12 words). Eliminate most articles and prepositions you might ordinarily use if the title were a sentence. Be sure to include the focus or topic of your study.

☐ Interact with peers, colleagues, and experts in your field throughout all phases of your work, from initial ideas to development of recommendations. Reviewing ideas with others will add richness to your study.

☐ Know the 'gurus' within your area of interest, and consider being personally in touch with one or more in your particular field of study to ask specific questions or to respond to ideas you may have for your study.

Remember to work smart. You do not have to read every book and journal article. Keep your purpose clearly in mind and use it to focus your search. Ask for assistance from your librarians. Also, the website, http://www.writing.utoronto.ca/advice/specific-types-of-writing/literature-review provides a helpful summary of how to write a Literature Review.

The following sections are examples of headings you might use in Chapter Two. Add headings and/or sub-headings as needed for your topic. Headings should appear in the same order as listed in the introductory paragraph(s).

Introduction – untitled

The introduction to Chapter Two provides a re-orientation to the purpose of the research study, and refers to the topics within the upcoming chapter. This introductory section will not have a heading. Chapter Two begins with the same purpose statement articulated in Chapter One: "The purpose of this study is to . . ." Use identical words for the purpose statement as were written in the purpose section of Chapter One. Then identify the topics to be discussed in Chapter Two: "In Chapter Two, a review of the literature includes a historical overview of . . . the current findings from . . . and [add remaining topics]."

The topics you list in the introduction to Chapter Two should appear as headings in the body of your Literature Review in the same order. Since each Literature Review is unique, your headings may be different from the examples given in this Guide. Select your headings from the outline of your Literature Review. The outlines that follow Figures 2.1 and 2.2 provide examples. The order of topics is from the global view (big picture) to the specific.

Note the use of tense for describing what others have said. Past tense is used for the Literature Review, for example Anderson (2017) report**ed,** stat**ed**. Other verbs and phrases you might find helpful as you report the findings and thoughts of other writers are listed in Table 2.1.

These words can be similarly effective when reporting a participant's comments in Chapter Four of a qualitative study.

Proof read your writing to ensure smooth transitions into quotes, and smooth transitions from one paragraph to the next (APA, 2010b).

Be careful to cite the source of direct quotes and of ideas expressed. Citations are an indicator you are showing respect for the ideas of others. Failure to cite sources – whether direct quotes, or others' ideas – is academic dishonesty, often referred

Table 2.1

Verbs/phrases for reporting findings

Described	Clarified
Made the point	Detailed how the process worked
Introduced the idea/notion	Stated clearly
Believed that	Commented
Suggested that	Reviewed the findings of
Argued for	Found
Another researcher argued that	Discovered
Observed that	Perceived
Continued by saying	Detailed how the process worked
Defined	Asserted
Reflected on	Insisted
Expressed concern	Carefully added
Reported	Documented
Underscored	Pointed out
Summarized	Postulated

to as plagiarism. Each university has a plagiarism policy, usually found in the general catalog. Citation of sources using APA formatting is modeled in this Guide, and hints for using citations are provided in this section. Additional information may be found in the *Publication Manual of the American Psychological Association* (APA, 2010b), and online at http://www. apastyle.org/

Historical overview of . . . and/or theories of . . . and/or purposes of . . .

Research topics will differ in terms of how they need to be discussed. Some lend themselves to a historical overview. Self-esteem is an example. It has been a foundational topic for psychological research since 1890 (Mruk, 2013). Identifying the roots of self-esteem and its development over time helps to set the context for the topic. Such writing would appear under the heading, Historical Overview of Self-Esteem.

Most topics need to be broken down by themes or sub-topics that contribute to an understanding of the larger picture. To use the example of self-esteem again, it would be helpful to present the various theories of self-esteem as shown in Figure 2.1. Differing perspectives or conflicting views of a topic contribute to a more complete view of the big picture. Another example of breaking a topic into sub-topics is with the subject of teacher supervision as shown in Figure 2.2. Here again, identifying different perspectives would be important.

In whatever way you design the organization of the Literature Review, craft it to present what is currently known about the topic from reliable sources, and show how your study fits within a bigger picture. In so doing, you will demonstrate your understanding of the topic. Be sure to include subheadings where possible to help guide the reader.

Current findings

Once the context for the study has been developed, a review and critique of research studies that have contributed to current knowledge will add to an overall understanding. Together, the context and recent findings will form the backdrop for your research proposal, and provide the framework that points to the need for your study. Keep your purpose clearly in mind – as though it were taped to your computer monitor! It is the guide for what literature you review and which methodology you choose. Be sure to identify controversies, conflicting views, and/or differing perspectives on a topic. Include subheadings where appropriate to help guide the reader. The headings should reflect the outline for the chapter.

Chapter summary

The summary for Chapter Two should provide a brief review of the literature and background information that supports answering the research question(s). The Literature Review should harmonize with the purpose of your study by pointing out the gaps in what is known about your topic and substantiate the need for your study.

As mentioned in the summary of Chapter One, the introductory part of each chapter tells what you are going to say; the body of the chapter says what you want to say; and the summary of the chapter says briefly what you have said. The summary of Chapter Two should end with a brief introduction to Chapter Three.

The next chapter in this Guide will distinguish between qualitative methodology, quantitative methodology, and Action Research, and briefly discuss the procedures needed for data collection.

For further Chapter Three information see Ary et al. (2006); Gall et al. (2006); Mertens (2015); Trochim and Donnelly (2007).

Methodology

Chapter Three of the Guide presents distinctions in research methodologies and identifies how the differences are reflected in the design of the research and in data collection. The chapter begins with a brief comparison of the philosophical paradigms from which qualitative and quantitative methodologies and Action Research flow. Each methodology is then outlined in order to describe the research design. Headings are suggested that might appear in Chapter Three of your study.

Chapter Three of your study will present the methodology you plan to use. Note that you will not proceed beyond describing your methodology to gathering data until you receive permission to proceed from the proposal stage. There are three general categories of research methodology used in education: qualitative research, quantitative research, and historical research. Survey research contains elements of both qualitative and quantitative paradigms. Action Research, which investigates one's practice, may use qualitative methodology, quantitative methodology, or a combination of both.

Each research design is a sub-category of empirical research, which seeks to gather information by observation and experimentation. Experimental studies are those in which there is random assignment of things or participants being studied. Quasi-experimental studies are those in which random assignment of things or participants is not practical or not possible.

Researchers usually choose a methodology based on the nature of the questions being asked; however, it is helpful to understand the philosophical paradigm and the assumptions at the root of a methodology. Patton (2015) recognized the longstanding debate about how best to conduct research; however, he also noted that an understanding of philosophical paradigms can help researchers choose a perspective most relevant to the problem they are investigating. Research is commonly approached through the Positivist/Postpositivist paradigm, the Constructivist paradigm, or the Pragmatic paradigm. A very concise explanation of these three main philosophical paradigms is provided here, as summarized from the perspectives of Ary et al. (2006); Creswell (2014); Gall et al. (2006); Mertens (2015); and Patton (2015). An understanding of these philosophical paradigms contributes to an understanding of the definitions of quantitative and qualitative methodologies.

Positivist/Postpositivist paradigm

The Positivist/Postpositivist paradigm assumes that laws govern human behavior in a way similar to how laws govern the physical world. It is therefore possible to derive testable theories to investigate human actions and relationships. Quantitative methodology is rooted in this paradigm. Researchers propose hypotheses, and use objective measurements and numerical analysis to determine relationships and to explain causes of change. Creswell (2014) defined a quantitative study as one that is "based on testing a theory composed of variables, measured with numbers, and analyzed with statistical procedures in order to determine whether the predictive generalizations of the theory hold true" (p. 2).

Constructivist paradigm

The Constructivist paradigm assumes that human behavior is bound to the context in which it occurs, and cannot be reduced to generalized laws that apply to all situations as is the case for findings in the physical sciences. Meaning is constructed inductively and holistically to understand human experience in a context specific setting (Merriam & Tisdell, 2016; Patton, 2015). Such is qualitative research. It begins *without* hypotheses. Researchers examine specific cases or cultures in natural settings, and use analysis of subjective data to gain understanding and then to possibly generate hypotheses. Qualitative researchers code and categorize data for the purpose of identifying themes that can be used to build a theory grounded in what they observe and hear. Ary et al. (2006) stated, "The ultimate goal of (qualitative) inquiry is to portray the complex pattern of what is being studied in sufficient depth and detail so that one who has not experienced it can understand it" (p. 476).

Pragmatic paradigm

In theory, the Positivist/Postpositivist and Constructivist approaches are philosophical opposites. In reality, researchers usually see value in both paradigms and choose the methodology that best suits the research questions they are asking. This approach represents the Pragmatic paradigm in which researchers choose a methodology based on the nature of the questions they ask rather than asking questions bound to a single paradigm.

Table 3.1 lists some of the attributes of the two methodologies most commonly used in educational research: qualitative methodology and quantitative methodology.

Table 3.1

Terminology, methods, and techniques of qualitative and quantitative research

Qualitative research	Quantitative research
Specific methodology may be: Ethnography, Phenomenology, Case study, Descriptive, Field research.	Specific methodology may be: Experimental, Quasi-experimental, or Pre-experimental.
Flexible design: Uses words to study human behavior that takes place in the context of lived experience. The researcher is the primary instrument for gathering data.	Concrete design: Aims at explanation that includes the discovery and use of laws. It uses objective measurement and numerical analysis to explain change.
Describes perceptions, experiences, what people say they believe, feelings they express, explanations they give.	Examines the measurable effects of a treatment, its attributes, differences, relationships, or changes over a period of time given some baseline data.
Focus is on understanding, describing, and discovering patterns directly tied to specific phenomena. Primarily uses inductive reasoning, moving from data towards a theory.	Focus is on explanation with an attempt to predict and generalize. Primarily uses deductive reasoning by investigating a hypothesis.
Understanding comes through analysis of narratives of "insiders" whose responses are categorized in themes, patterns, and commonalities.	Explanation comes through measurement, analysis, and description of numbers through measurable data using descriptive statistics and inferential statistics.

(*Continued*)

Table 3.1 *Continued*

Interviews and observations are sources of data for analysis. An interview may begin with these types of questions: Tell me about . . . Can you give me an example of . . . Would you clarify or expand on . . .	Dependent and independent variables are given numerical value. Numerical analysis is used to explain change: The *dependent variable* is being investigated. Change may occur as a result of another variable(s). The *independent variable* is a factor shown hypothesized to have an influence on the dependent variable.
Reports present the natural language of participants drawn from interview data and documents.	Reports present tables of statistics, graphs to display numerical data.
See Ary et al. (2006); Gall et al. (2006); Mertens (2015).	See Ary et al. (2006); Gall et al. (2006); Mertens (2015).

Action Research.

One of the variants of the Pragmatic paradigm is Action Research. Action Research is a solution-oriented process through which practitioners investigate practical problems for the purpose of making data driven decisions and improving their own practice. Action Research is solution-oriented, merging theory and practice. It is a way for practitioners to systematically observe, gather and analyze data, and provide evidence of what works rather than relying on intuition or guessing. Educators who carry out Action Research are modeling the kind of learning they would ultimately like to see in their students. Gay, Mills, and Airasian (2012) described Action Research as a method of investigating one's practice using systematic, purposeful inquiry.

As shown in Figure 3.1, the Action Research cycle begins with identification of a particular problem that has arisen in daily practice.

Example of qualitative research question (from Chapter One): *What are the perceptions and expectations of M&M's® consumers about the colors and quantities of candies in a box of M&M's®?*

Example of quantitative research question (from Chapter One): *What is the numerical relationship between the number of each color of candies in a box of M&M's® and the total number of candies?*

The cycle continues with an investigation of literature about past or current approaches to the problem, generates a plan for investigating the issue, implements the plan through collection of data, analyzes the data, and moves forward with informed recommendations and action. The research design may be qualitative, constructing meaning from interviews, observations, and reflections; quantitative, in which procedures are used to measure and record change; or survey methodology, which might mean gathering a combination of qualitative and quantitative data.

Action researchers need to be aware that some tools they may employ, such as self-generated surveys or inventories, may lack validity and reliability. In general, the *validity* of a measuring instrument is demonstrated when it can be shown in various

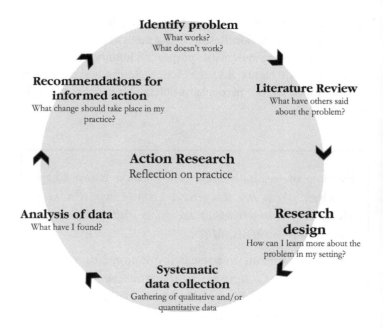

Identify problem
What works?
What doesn't work?

Recommendations for informed action
What change should take place in my practice?

Literature Review
What have others said about the problem?

Action Research
Reflection on practice

Analysis of data
What have I found?

Research design
How can I learn more about the problem in my setting?

Systematic data collection
Gathering of qualitative and/or quantitative data

Figure 3.1 Model for Action Research

ways that the instrument is measuring what we think it is measuring. The *reliability* of an instrument is shown when similar results are consistently obtained time after time when the same instrument is used to measure the same characteristics of similar groups. If self-generated measuring tools are used, the lack of proven validity and reliability must be noted as one of the limits to the study (see Chapter One, Delimitations). Use of personally designed surveys does not mean their use in Action Research lacks meaning as long as the limitations of their use are understood and noted. Strategies for strengthening the reliability and validity of studies and of self-generated tools are addressed in upcoming discussions of particular headings that might appear in each methodology.

Validity: *The right things were consistently measured. Boxes of identical size were always used by those who counted the number and color of M&M's®.*

Reliability: *The results are consistently the same. When the M&M's® counters reported the number of candies in identically sized boxes, the count was consistently the same.*

Further information on Action Research may be found at http://www.aral.com.au/resources/arphome.html

Content of Chapter Three

Chapter Three can be likened to creating a recipe in that it should be easily understood and followed. Chapter Three should contain enough information to assure the reader that you have followed established research conventions and enable a reader to replicate the study. It lays out your plan for conducting research so that it is open to scrutiny. The research design should answer questions such as: What type of methodology will be used? What will be the sources of information? How will the site be selected? How will the population be defined? Who will participate in the study? What will be the criteria for selection? How will the sample be selected? Will the sample be random, systematic, one of convenience, or purposeful? Will the data be confidential or anonymous? Procedures for obtaining permission from participants and for maintaining confidentiality or anonymity of data need to be discussed regardless of methodology. The research planning guide in Table 3.1 provides prompts for each of the questions posed.

Examples of headings in Chapter Three

The following sections show examples of headings you might use in Chapter Three. Note that headings used for qualitative methodology will be different than those used for quantitative methodology. Add headings and/or sub-headings as needed to describe the methodology for your specific study.

Introduction – untitled.

Introduce Chapter Three with an introductory sentence or short paragraph. This introductory section will not have a heading. It may begin with: "The purpose of this study is to . . . Chapter Three will present the (qualitative or quantitative) methodology that will be employed to answer the research question(s) presented in Chapter One: . . ." Chapter Three is written in the future tense because the gathering of data has not yet been done. Within the introduction, introduce the topics that you will present in the chapter.

Research design.

Begin the Research Design section with a statement about the type of study you will conduct (qualitative, quantitative, or Action Research), and an explanation of why the method was chosen. Then use sub-headings to address the needed elements of your research design.

Qualitative methodology, also known as naturalistic inquiry, is designed to search for understanding of themes, patterns, or causal explanations through the lived experience of the study participants. It presents explanations based on the perspective of an insider. Qualitative methodology *does not* use hypotheses or assumptions, though these may be generated by the findings.

A quantitative study, on the other hand, begins with a theory or hypothesis to be investigated. Numerical data are gathered and analyzed to determine whether the hypothesis can be supported, and whether explanation may be provided by way of generalization or prediction.

This Guide discusses the specifics and headings of qualitative and quantitative design studies in the following sections, as well as those for an Action Research study.

A tool to assist in organizing the components of the research design is found in Table 3.2. Particularly helpful as a summary, the document provides a snapshot of the details that must be attended to as the study is planned.

Headings for a qualitative design study.
The methodology section of a qualitative research study explains clearly how the research design will accomplish the purpose of the study. Headings that may be needed for a study that uses qualitative design include site selection, participant selection, role of the researcher, data selection, building dependability, and data analysis.

Site selection.
Describe the general location and demographic characteristics of the site you chose for your study. Do not identify the specific geographic location or name of the site without permission. A description such as "a school district in Southern California" locates where a study was carried out, and is sufficiently general so that the specific site is not identified. Provide the background needed that sets the stage for your study to take place.

Participant selection.
Describe how you chose the study participants from a larger group of possible participants. Note that interviews in qualitative research are likely to produce large amounts of data, and therefore the number of participants should be limited to keep

Table 3.2

Research planning guide

Title _____
Purpose The purpose of the study is to _____
Literature Review/Rationale of study Context for study in light of existing scholarship
Methodology and **data analysis** **Research methods** ☐ Quantitative ☐ Qualitative ☐ Action Research **Data collection/Measuring instrument** ☐ Online Survey ☐ Paper Survey ☐ Existing Data ☐ Test Measures ☐ Inventory ☐ Interviews ☐ Focus Group **Rationale:** _____ ☐ **Data will be confidential** (recorded so that data are not readily identified with the participant, but such a link is possible through coding or unique identifiers. Coding provides participants' identity, but the two are kept separate). ☐ **Data will be anonymous** (recorded so that data can never be linked to specific participants). **Population and sample size** Criteria for Population Selection: _____ Population Size: _____ Sample Size: _____ Sample Size Calculator: http://www.surveysystem.com/sscalc.htm#cineeded Location(s): _____ _____ _____ _____ **Data analysis/Variables** For quantitative data: ☐ Gender ☐ Ethnicity ☐ Age   ☐ Location ☐ Other: For qualitative data: _____

Research schedule
Anticipated time for data collection: From DD/MM/YY _____   To DD/MM/YY _____ ☐ Cover letter/Invitation   ☐ Letter of consent   to participate ☐ Plan for pilot   ☐ Pilot completed
Approval   ☐ Faculty Advisor or Committee Chair   ☐ IRB
Budget

the study manageable. For this reason, few qualitative studies conducted by individual researchers have more than six participants. Surveys are likely to have many more participants because the data gathered are focused and more limited in nature.

In choosing the participants, purposive sampling may be needed so that the group is representative of the characteristics needed to accomplish the purpose of the study (Gall et al., 2006; Mertens, 2015).

Role of the researcher.

As an interviewer, you are the primary instrument for gathering data (Merriam & Tisdell, 2016). Describe your relationship to the participants and how your interest and experience led you to become involved in conducting the study. Identify the overarching interview question(s) you will ask the participants, and refine them by posing the questions to people who are similar to the participants but who will not be part of your study. When you are certain the overarching questions are clear and free of ambiguity, create a list of prompting questions that could be used as needed during interviews. These prompting questions need not be included in Chapter Three but should be part of your notes for the interview process.

Data collection and triangulation.

Use of multiple sources of data and/or methods of data collection is called triangulation. It is important to use triangulation as a way of strengthening the credibility and trustworthiness of the study. Describe the different strategies or procedures in which you will collect data.

Triangulation compares the findings from various sources to look for similarities in observations in more than one data source and thus lends credibility to the findings (Ary et al., 2006; Gay et al., 2012). Sources of data may include:

- Interviews of participants, which are usually recorded and transcribed. Plan for a quiet place, sufficient time, and needed recording equipment.
- A focus group, which is a group interview involving all of the participants. Focus group participants are invited to make sense of the data collected from interviews and share their insights. The researcher gains additional understanding by asking questions of the group and noting the responses and interactions.
- Documents the participants have created, and which are related to the purpose of the study.

Triangulation enhances the credibility and trustworthiness of a study. Different strategies or procedures for data collection are used to establish or confirm whether the data collected in one way confirms data collected in a different way. If the findings from multiple sources agree, triangulation of data has occurred, and the accuracy and credibility of findings are enhanced. Triangulation is a technique of value in the design of both qualitative and quantitative studies.

Building dependability.

The dependability of data and findings is enhanced by use of strategies such as member checks and an audit trail. A member check occurs when the researcher asks individual participants whether the researcher has accurately described and interpreted what the member said. An audit trail is a collection of documents that other researchers may ask to see. These documents show the researcher's procedures, reflections, and participant data. Allowing others to scrutinize the audit trail is a way to build dependability into the study.

Data analysis.

Data analysis in qualitative research begins in the field even as data are being gathered as the researcher listens and observes. Analysis continues with the major tasks of organizing and coding information gathered from transcripts of interviews, notes from the focus group, and other documents. Masses of data must be distilled into categories that represent themes and patterns. Reading and re-reading of transcript data will be needed to search for meaning and relationships.

Summary.

A brief, 'say what you said' summary should complete the chapter. The summary of Chapter Three should end with a brief introduction to Chapter Four.

Headings for a quantitative design study.

As with the methodology section of a qualitative study, the methodology section for a quantitative study clearly explains how the research will be designed to accomplish the purpose of the study. Headings needed to outline quantitative methodology may include the setting and the population being considered, the treatment (if any) you will administer, the measuring instruments or other sources of data, procedures for conducting the study, how the data will be analyzed, and other information relevant to conducting the study (Ary et al., 2006).

The setting and the population.

Describe the general location and demographic characteristics of the site you chose for your study. Do not identify the specific geographic location or name of the site without permission. Provide the background needed for why you have chosen a specific location.

Describe the target population and the sample of the population about whom you will gather data. Explain how you will select the sample from the larger group. Selection may be random or purposeful, depending on the purpose of the study and practicality.

The treatment.

Carefully describe the treatment you or others will administer to the sample population. The treatment should be described in sufficient detail to provide guidance for others to replicate the study. Documents essential to the treatment, such as lesson plans or reading materials, should be included in an appendix.

Measuring instruments and other sources of data.

Describe any research instruments you will use such as tests or inventories. If the instrument is already established, report on its reliability and validity. Should you need to make up your own test instrument, describe how you will address the issues of reliability and validity. For example, an instrument you design should be piloted with people similar to your sample population to see whether results are what you might expect. Findings from the piloted instrument will help to build data on reliability and validity of the instrument. In addition, have others who are experts in your area of investigation examine the test instrument, and invite their input.

Some sources of data are historical in nature, and may be obtained through databases or student records. Describe where you will get the information and the protocol you will follow for permission to access the data.

For some types of data gathering, you may need to develop your own questionnaire or survey. A good survey makes three things very clear for respondents: First, a description of what is being measured must be clear. For example, the initial information might say, "The purpose of this survey is to learn about respondents' perceptions of Help Desk Support."

Second, respondents need to know clearly what it is that you want to learn about what is being measured. Provide a description about the items about which you are asking. For example, to learn about 'Help Desk Support', the survey might say, "We want to find your perceptions of the *quality* or *ease of use* of Help Desk service." Additional descriptions listed in Table 3.3 provide examples of other things you might want to learn about the item being measured:

Third, the data gathered will be more useful if we know clearly the respondents' level of awareness of specific services, which services they have used, importance of the service, satisfaction,

Table 3.3

Attributes that might be assessed

Quality	Timeliness
Ease of use	Instruction
Value	Reliability
Accessibility	Efficiency
Accuracy	Courtesy
Relevance	Knowledge
Extent of personal interaction	Degree of professionalism
Understanding of needs	Other attributes of interest

or similar terms. Examples of how such questions may be asked include the following.

- *Awareness*: Please indicate which of the following services you are aware of.
- *Services used*: For each of the following services that you are aware of, please indicate which ones you have used in the last year.
- *Rating of the service*: For each of the following services you have used in the last year, please rate how useful you find each service.
- *Importance of the service*: Please rate how important each of the following services are to you.
- *Satisfaction*: For each of these same services, please rate how satisfied you are with each service.

A widely used survey format was developed by Rensis Likert. Likert created a scale for responding to prompts that use categories such as "strongly agree", "agree", "disagree", and "strongly disagree". Note that in this example, neutral categories are not used because the researcher may want to avoid a neutral response. However, for some purposes researchers may use a neutral or undecided choice so that respondents are not forced into agreeing or disagreeing with an item. Frequently, responses are assigned a numeric value: "strongly agree = 4, agree = 3" and so on. Respondents' answers can then be numerically summarized.

We strongly recommend that each number or category of a scale be defined. For example, if a five-point scale is required, each category should be defined so that decisions about specific ratings are not left entirely to respondents. Respondents should know how a rating of "5" differs from the rating of a "4" or "3". When a scale is defined, respondents have guidance upon which to make their ratings, and reliability of the findings is strengthened. Clear and unambiguous questions combined with clearly defined rating scales contribute to the reliability and validity of the instrument. This means that very similar results are likely to be obtained when the instrument is repeatedly given to the same population in the same way at different times, or when the instrument is given by different survey administrators. Ultimately, affirmative responses to the questions, "Does the survey measure what we intend to measure?" and, "Does it do so consistently with similar populations?" contribute to meaningful findings. An example illustrating survey planning, design and construction, methodology, survey results, and data analysis can be found in Germaine & Kornuta (2009).

Further reliability and validity can be established by constructing multiple questions on the same issue to determine if respondents' answers are consistent. Having survey instruments reviewed and critiqued by other experts can also strengthen validity. Piloting the survey with a population similar to, but different from, those who you want to participate in your study will strengthen validity. The results of piloting a survey may indicate whether something is missing, something needs to be added, or whether some questions are unclear.

Similarly, the process of constructing multiple questions to strengthen validity of survey data parallels the strategy of data triangulation in the qualitative design section of this chapter.

Procedures for conducting the study.
State the hypothesis for the study and the steps you will follow to observe whether or not the hypothesis is true. Be as clear and precise as possible in your description so that others who read the procedure may replicate the study.

Data analysis.
The data analysis section describes how you will organize and present data, and describes the statistical procedures you will

use. Descriptive statistics may be used to summarize data in tables, charts, and graphs. The procedure chosen for inferential statistics should be selected on the basis of its appropriateness in answering the research question.

Several terms are important to descriptive statistics. The mean, median, and mode are measures of central tendency. The standard deviation indicates the spread of scores. Individually, these measures provide snapshots of specific information; when used in conjunction with one another, a more accurate picture of the distribution of scores can be communicated. To support the understanding of terms used in descriptive statistics, the measures of central tendency (mean, median, and mode) and measure of variance (standard deviation) are defined in Table 3.4 with example calculations provided.

Summary.
A brief, 'say what you said' summary of the quantitative design should complete the chapter. The summary of Chapter Three should end with a brief introduction to Chapter Four.

Headings for an Action Research study.
As noted earlier, Action Research is a methodology in which researchers investigate their own practice by reflecting on what they do, identifying a question or problem, exploring what others have done, planning and implementing change, and documenting the results. The headings in reporting about an Action Research study would parallel the headings in either of the qualitative or quantitative sections discussed above.

Summary.
A brief, 'say what you said' summary of the Action Research study design should complete the chapter. The summary of Chapter Three should end with a brief introduction to Chapter Four.

Measures of central tendency and measures of variance

Term	Definition	Example calculations
Mean	The arithmetic average: divide the sum of all scores by the number of responses.	Example scores: 1 2 2 3 3 4 4 4 4 5 Mean = $\dfrac{1+2+2+3+3+4+4+4+4+5}{10}$ = 3.2
Median	The point that divides a distribution of scores in half.	Example scores: 1 2 2 3 3 4 4 4 4 5 In this list of even scores, the median is the midpoint between each group of five scores. The value in the middle is 3.5. If there were 11 scores in the example, the middle number (the sixth number) would be the median.
Mode	The most common or frequent score in a set of scores.	Example scores: 1 2 2 3 3 4 4 4 4 5 In this list of scores, the most frequently occurring score, or the mode, is 4.
Standard deviation (SD)	A measure of how tightly or widely individual scores are spread apart from the mean. A large SD occurs when scores are widely spread apart. A small SD indicates the scores are closely clustered together.	Example scores: 1 2 2 3 3 4 4 4 4 5

Standard deviation example table:

Column 1 Ten scores	Column 2 Deviation of score from mean	Column 3 Squares of deviation scores
X	x	x^2
1	-2.2	4.84

(Continued)

Table 3.4 Continued

Term	Definition	Example calculations
	Standard Deviation is calculated by taking the square root of the sum of the squares of the deviation scores (Column 3) and dividing by the total number of scores (Column 1). The standard deviation formula is $$\sqrt{\sum} = \frac{x^2}{X}$$	**Column**

Column	1 Ten scores	2 Deviation of score from mean	3 Squares of deviation scores
	X	x	x^2
	2	-1.2	1.44
	2	-1.2	1.44
	3	-0.2	0.04
	3	-0.2	0.04
	4	0.8	0.64
	4	0.8	0.64
	4	0.8	0.64
	4	0.8	0.64
	5	1.8	3.24
Sum	32		13.6 $Sum(x^2)$
Mean	3.2		

Standard deviation calculation:

$$\sqrt{\frac{13.6}{10}} = 1.17$$

The value of 1.17 indicates how widely the scores are spread apart. The average amount that a score deviates

Chapter summary

Overall, the summary for Chapter Three should provide a brief review of the methodology that supports fulfilling the purpose of the study and answers the research question(s). No new information should appear in the summary. As mentioned in the summary of Chapters One and Two, the introductory part of each chapter tells what you are going to say; the body of the chapter says what you want to say; and the summary of the chapter says briefly what you have said.

For further information about the topics in Chapter Three, see Ary et al. (2006); Gall et al. (2006); Gay et al. (2012); Mertens (2015).

Findings and analysis

This chapter provides suggestions for presenting data gathered from your research and analyzing the information. This chapter begins by describing what is needed in the introductory section of Chapter Four of your research study, proposes sample headings that might appear throughout your chapter when reporting either qualitative data or quantitative data, and provides specific descriptions of what might be written under the sample headings.

Developing an outline is an important step in preparing the presentation of the analysis of findings. Major ideas become clear as you search for a logical structure and layout of the data. An outline also provides a guide for headings to use throughout the chapter. Chapter Four begins with an introductory section (without a heading), which restates the purpose of the study and identifies what is to come in the chapter. The following is an example of how the introduction of Chapter Four might be written:

> The purpose of this study was to determine if there was a statistically significant difference in measures of self-esteem between elementary school students to whom specific values

were formally taught as part of the curriculum, and those who did not receive such instruction. A review of the theories of self-esteem identified self-esteem to be a dynamic inter-relationship of feelings of competence and worthiness.

The chapter begins with a summary of the purpose of the study and a description of the methodology. It then examines the results of data collection and provides analysis in light of the two research questions and the five hypotheses. The story is told about how the sample population was chosen, how data for the variables was reported, and continues by presenting results and analysis of multiple regression models.

(Germaine, 2001, p. 82)

Chapter Four of a research study is written in the past tense since data have been gathered and analyzed. Note that after the proposal section (Chapters One, Two and Three) has been approved and the research carried out, the first three chapters are re-written in past tense.

Headings common to both qualitative and quantitative studies

The first heading in Chapter Four for both qualitative and quantitative studies should be Background and Setting. Each chapter of a research study contributes to the whole, but at the same time each chapter should stand on its own. Therefore, a brief description of the background and setting of the study should also be included in Chapter Four. The following is an example of how the background and setting of a study might be reported:

The participants in this qualitative study were teachers in a school district that has two supervision programs: a nonevaluative developmental supervision model and an evaluative performance appraisal model. Once every five years, the principal and teacher meet to agree on completing one of the two programs. Developmental supervision is generally chosen if the teacher does not require, or has not requested, a performance appraisal.

The developmental supervision program is intended to facilitate ongoing teacher development. Teachers or principals may initiate this supervisory process. They meet early in the fall for an orientation at which time a plan is jointly developed to personalize the process. Teachers identify an area where growth is required, and together, the teacher and principal determine goals. Options for data collection include the portfolio project. With this option, teachers proceed to collect data, and monthly conferences are planned for reflection and interaction. This supervisory program recognizes teachers' professionalism, nurtures critical and creative thinking, and encourages professional reading. The completed project is submitted to the superintendent.

The participants in this study chose the portfolio project for their developmental supervision. They heard about this option at a fall staff meeting and those interested in the portfolio option attended a small group information session. Participants asked clarifying questions and listened to testimonials from teachers at their school who spoke about their experience, shared their completed portfolio projects, and offered to provide support.

(Kornuta, 2001, p. 64)

Table 4.1 shows the types of headings that might be used in reporting qualitative and quantitative results.

Table 4.1

Qualitative and quantitative headings that may be used for Chapter Four

Sample qualitative headings	*Sample quantitative headings*
Background and Setting Choosing Participants Summary of Findings. Sub-headings in this section may include: • a report of findings by participant; • research and interview questions; • time; • themes and/or other topic organizers Summary	Background and Setting Choosing the Sample Population Demographics. Describe the demographics of the population. If there are two or more groups, show a demographic comparison. Variables and Measures of Variables Statistical Procedure Review of Hypotheses or Discussion of Results Summary

Headings for qualitative findings and analysis

The following points provide specific descriptions of what might be written within the headings suggested in Table 4.1.

Background and setting.

Briefly review the background and setting for the study. The example in the headings section of this chapter indicates how the setting and context of a study might be reported.

Choosing participants.

Describe how and why the participants in the study were selected. For example:

> The following criteria guided participant selection: teachers who had most recently completed their project as part of their developmental supervision; teachers actively teaching in the elementary school setting with children from kindergarten to grade 8; and teachers who had at least five years of teaching experience. Eight teachers were contacted; two declined due to previous professional commitments.
>
> (Kornuta, 2001, p. 49)

Summary of findings.

Chapter Four begins the formal presentation of the analysis of data. However, for researchers gathering qualitative data, interpretation and analysis of data begin with the first interview. Through careful listening, observing, and reflecting, preliminary patterns may emerge, and these patterns themselves may shape some of the data gathered. Interview questions are often used as organizers for analyzing qualitative data. It is important to represent and communicate fairly what the data revealed. Qualitative data should be presented in detailed descriptions with direct quotations used to capture the perspectives and experiences of the participants.

Each qualitative study is unique and therefore the analysis for each study will be distinctive and depend greatly on the researcher's practice, experiences, and analytical style. In qualitative research, the challenge is to integrate data sources that become part of the analysis. As integration occurs, significant patterns within the data sources result in the formation of themes.

Participants in the study should be asked to verify transcripts of their response to interview questions. This process is called a member check. It is an important step, which verifies that the transcript captured what the participant said, and in so doing adds reliability to the findings. The interview transcripts are ana-lyzed for themes, and themes common to each participant are identified.

Data from other sources (field notes, participant journals, focus group data) are analyzed and integrated with interview data as a way of strengthening the validity and reliability of the find-ings. The process of combining data from two or more sources is called triangulation. When data from two or more sources show agreement, the findings are strengthened. When data from two or more sources differ, questions about the methodology and/or findings are raised, or unanticipated insights gained.

Within the section headed by Summary of Findings, other sub-headings will be needed. Analysis of findings may be orga-nized and reported by one or more of the following groupings.

Participants.
A summary of the findings should be given for each interview with each participant. Include direct quotations from the participants in their exact language. The following is an example of how a direct quote was used in reporting findings in a qualitative study:

> Gail benefited from collegial collaboration in her role as librarian in three schools; challenging situations developed her problem-solving ability. She proudly stated, "The port-folio allowed me to think about what I was doing and how I was doing it; that has now become a pattern in the way I operate." She gained affirmation that she was successfully fulfilling her role as teacher librarian, which increased her sense of competence.
>
> (Kornuta, 2001, p. 69)

Research and interview questions.
Summarize the data by research and interview questions. In this type of data summary, individual interview responses are pooled

and organized by interview question to present what participants said collectively. Organization by question may be particularly relevant for Action Research and qualitative studies that use surveys as part of data gathering. Tables or figures or both, as needed, are effective in succinctly communicating results by question. Refer to the tables or figures within the text to point out important details. Full descriptions of tables and figures in the text are not needed or the table or figure itself may be redundant.

Time.

Chronological order may be used to describe responses over time if 'time' is relevant to organizing the data.

Themes or topics.

From the summary of data, present the patterns that emerge as themes or topics. Data are grouped according to what is significant and meaningful, and patterns are sought based on commonalities and differences.

Summary.

Use the headings as a guide to outline and summarize what you have said in Chapter Four. Provide a sentence or two that bridges Chapter Four to Chapter Five.

For specific methods of analyzing qualitative data, see Ary et al. (2006); Gall et al. (2006); Mertens (2015).

Headings for quantitative findings and analysis

Quantitative data need to be summarized and presented accurately, clearly, and succinctly. Tables and figures are used to condense the data and provide initial explanation. Reference to each table or figure should be made within the text. Such commentary provides additional insight, pointing out the most important and interesting features. Begin the presentation of data with general demographic information, and then use the hypotheses as an organizer (or organizers) for presenting the findings of the study. Statistical procedures are then explained, and tables, figures, and commentary are used to describe and provide verification for the findings. Avoid going into mathematical detail. Where such explanation is necessary, place it in footnotes or in an appendix to avoid interrupting the flow of reporting the findings.

The following provides specific descriptions of what might be written within the sample headings.

Background and setting.
Briefly review the background and setting for the study. The following is an example:

> The setting for the study was a Canadian school district that had identified a set of values through community consensus. In addition, they had prepared curriculum and lesson plans, and had instituted a values education program for a period of four years. Initiative for the program came jointly from school district leadership, teachers, and parents. Workshops were held to introduce the curriculum to teachers, to encourage them to model the values, and to suggest they integrate discussion of values throughout other curricula.
>
> (Germaine, 2001, p. 83)

Choosing the sample population.
State how and why the sample was chosen from the larger population, and use tables as needed to present information about the control and treatment groups. For example:

> An important task in addressing the research questions and hypotheses was to select students who had been taught the

values education curriculum, and a demographically similar group of students who had not been taught the curriculum. I met with two members of the school district office to enlist their help in identifying two such groups. As a result, a letter was sent to over forty elementary school principals. The letter expressed school district support for the study and requested principals' help in identifying students who would fit into one of the two groups. Four administrators responded. They identified groups of students, and the teachers who could be contacted to ask about participating in the study.

Students from four schools became part of the sample population. The control group is larger because schools from this group each had two participating classes. The schools in the treatment group both contributed one class. All students in the treatment group had been exposed to the values education program from 4th grade through 7th grade.

(Germaine, 2001, p.86)

Demographics of the population.

Demographic information is the type of information available in a census. Describe demographics relevant to your study such as age, gender, and education level. Income level, marital status, religion, occupation, and other categories may also be relevant depending on the nature of the study. For example, a study of university alumni would likely include the year of graduation as important demographic information.

Variables and measures of variables.

Indicate what the dependent and independent variables were and describe how they were measured. Dependent and independent variables are given numerical value. The *dependent variable* is being investigated; change may occur as a result of another variable(s). The *independent variable* is a factor shown or hypothesized by way of the Literature Review to have an influence on the dependent variable. Numerical analysis is used to explain change. Provide tables as needed to summarize the data. The description of variables in the next paragraph is from a study that investigated the effect on students' self-esteem when values were explicitly taught in the classroom. Self-esteem was therefore the dependent variable, and influences that correlated with self-esteem (independent variables) needed to be identified as did ways of measuring such independent variables. For example:

> Part of the task in answering the research question was to identify, by way of literature review, variables that have some correlation to self-esteem in a school setting. Academic success, gender, behavior, values, physical appearance, social groupings, and physical abilities were found in the literature to be factors that contributed to self-esteem. The literature identified the home as having the greatest impact on self-esteem; however, measures were available only for students' academic success, gender, behavior, and whether or not values had been explicitly taught in school.
>
> (Germaine, 2001, p. 84)

Some explanation was then provided about how the dependent and independent variables were measured. Variables such as gender can be assigned numbers such as 0 for males and 1 for females.

Statistical procedure.

Describe how the data were analyzed. Use tables and figures as needed to present the results of analysis. Refer to the tables and figures in the text of writing as the results are explained. Use sufficient text to point out the most important and interesting findings (Ary et al., 2006). Do not include detailed mathematical explanations within the text of Chapter Four. Let the presentation of data and description of the analysis be the focus of the story you tell. Use footnotes or an appendix to provide mathematical detail. The following is a brief excerpt from a study:

> Since numerical data were available and the purpose of the study included determining the extent of relationships among variables, multiple regression analysis was chosen as the appropriate analytical tool to aid in the investigation. The plan for data analysis included determining a post-treatment measure of self-esteem using the Student Self-Esteem Inventory; then, using post-treatment data for each independent variable, determine relationships from the best fitting multiple regression model.
>
> Even though the control and treatment groups were demographically similar, enough difference existed to warrant the estimation of a pre-treatment measure of self-esteem with which to determine the change in self-esteem over the course of the values education program. Obtaining this estimate was accomplished by combining correlation coefficients from the post-treatment model, with historical pre-treatment data in a regression equation.
>
> (Germaine, 2001, p. 85)

Review of hypothesis or discussion of results.
Organize the report of your findings around each hypothesis. State whether null hypotheses can be rejected or should be retained. Negative results – results that do not provide the findings for which you hoped - may be disappointing, but they should be treated with as much respect as more positive results. An example of addressing negative results is illustrated through the following comments:

> The model as a whole accounted for only 6 per cent of the variation in self-esteem . . . Does the finding of no statistical

significance of the treatment on self-esteem mean that the values education program was ineffective? The emphatic answer is no. What it does mean is that the data used in this study in an attempt to link self-esteem with values education in the lives of elementary school children, may not have been precise or accurate measures of the outcomes of the program. In addition, variables known to influence self-esteem (home, family, physical abilities) and for which we had no measures may have masked the impact of the values education program ...

Theories of self-esteem summarized in the literature review showed a dynamic relationship between competence and worthiness, with social and personal values imbedded in each concept. . . . The results of this study do not change that theory. We are ill advised to state that the teaching of values was ineffective in the lives of children. The need remains to capture data that better indicate the relationship between values and self-esteem, identify settings and circumstances that better capture the results of teaching values, or identify more effective ways of transmitting values to children.

(Germaine, 2001, p. 106)

We strongly urge practitioners to plan a strategy for assessing the effectiveness of an intervention prior to initiating the intervention. Such a plan is likely to include valuable pre-measures, which may not be readily accessible at a later date. Planning for evaluation may even shape the intervention in a way that makes the assessment findings more meaningful.

Summary.
Use the headings as a guide to summarize what you have said in Chapter Four. Provide a sentence or two that bridges this chapter to Chapter Five.

Chapter summary

The summary for Chapter Four should provide a brief review of your results and analysis using the headings as a guide to say what you have said. As mentioned in the summary of other chapters, the introductory part of each chapter tells what you are going to say; the body of the chapter says what you want to say; and the summary of the chapter says briefly what you have said.

For further information on the topics discussed in Chapter Four, see Ary et al. (2006); Gall et al. (2006); Mertens (2015).

Summary, discussion of findings and conclusions, and recommendations

This chapter provides suggestions for concluding your study. Each chapter of a research study contributes to the whole, but at the same time each chapter should stand on its own. Some readers will focus on only one chapter, so a brief description of the background and setting of the study will bring greater meaning and understanding. Chapter Five of a research study is like an executive summary of your work. Those who read only Chapter Five should know the essence of what was said in the previous chapters. Chapter Five of a study looks back to summarize information presented in previous chapters; it discusses the study, identifies implications from the findings, and may draw inferences from the findings. Chapter Five also presents conclusions, looks ahead to provide recommendations for change in policy or practice, and suggests the need for further study.

Begin Chapter Five with an untitled, introductory section that includes the purpose of the study and a description of what is to come in the chapter. Headings would then reflect a summary of the previous chapters, extending to a discussion of findings, interpretation of results, recommendations for change and future study, and conclusions.

Headings for Chapter Five

As with previous chapters, begin with an untitled introduction. The headings shown below provide examples what might be needed.

Background and setting

Briefly review the background and setting for the study as described in Chapter One.

Methodology and research design.
This section summarizes the methodology addressed in Chapter Three. Review why you chose the specific design for your study. What literature supports the design and methodology you chose? It may be necessary to summarize findings from the Chapter Two Review of Literature to show support for the use of particular independent variables.

Discussion of findings and conclusions.
The discussion of findings reviews and expands on what has been learned as a direct result of the study as described in Chapter Four. And a reality is that the findings from a study may raise as many questions as they answer, and therefore lead to recommendations for further study.

Findings for each research question should be summarized separately. How has what you have found contributed to knowledge in the general field of study? Were the findings what you expected? If not, what factors may have contributed to the unexpected? Did an intervention result in no change? If it did, what factors might explain the lack of change? The finding of 'no change' in a study does not mean failure on the part of the researcher. Such a finding can be an important contribution to the field of study. Are there recommendations you might include for researchers who replicate your study or investigate further? Are there factors you did not anticipate that you suggest they consider? Is there a need for further study to expand on what you found?

Clear and logical reasoning should be evident. Conclusions are inferences based on the results of the study and *must* be clearly linked to findings. The task of researchers is to add to knowledge by analyzing data, explaining the results within relevant context, and making inferences and appropriate recommendations that link directly to findings.

Recommendations.

Recommendations may include suggestions for change in policy or practice based on the findings of the study, and may include recommendations for further study. Do not include recommendations that have no direct link to findings. Some insights from the study may indirectly imply the need for change; however, discussion of such insights should be within the context of the need for further study rather than for change in policy or practice.

Summary.

The summary for Chapter Five should provide a brief review of the chapter using the headings as a guide to say what you have said. As mentioned in the summary of other chapters, the introductory part of each chapter tells what you are going to say; the body of the chapter says what you want to say; and the summary of the chapter says briefly what you have said.

Chapter summary

Chapter Five has identified headings appropriate to the content for the chapter.

References

American Psychological Association (APA). (2010a). *Mastering APA style: Student's workbook and training guide* (6th ed.). Washington, DC: American Psychological Association.

American Psychological Association (APA). (2010b). *Publication manual of the American Psychological Association* (6th ed.). Washington, DC: American Psychological Association.

Ary, D., Jacobs, L.C., Razavieh, A., & Sorensen, C. (2006). *Introduction to research in education* (7th ed.). Fort Worth, TX: Harcourt Brace College Publishers.

Burns, J. (1978). *Leadership*. New York: Harper & Row.

Clark, V.L., & Creswell, J.W. (2010). *Understanding research: A consumer's guide*. Upper Saddle River, NJ: Pearson Education Inc.

Creswell, J.W. (2014). *Research design: Qualitative and quantitative approaches* (4th ed.). Thousand Oaks, CA: Sage Publications.

Dewey, J. (1916). *Democracy and education: An introduction to the philosophy of education*. New York: Macmillan.

Gall, M.D., Gall, J.P., & Borg, W.R. (2006). *Educational research: An introduction* (8th ed.). White Plains, NY: Longman.

Gay, L., Mills, G., & Airasian, P. (2012). *Educational research: Competencies for analysis and applications* (10th ed.). Upper Saddle River, NJ: Pearson Education, Inc.

Germaine, R. (2001). Values education influence on elementary students' self-esteem. *Dissertation Abstracts International, 62*(03). (UMI No. 3007290)

Germaine, R., & Kornuta, H. (2009, Summer). Perceptions of graduate student learning via a program exit survey. *AIR Professional File, 112.* Tallahassee, FL: Association for Institutional Research.

Greene, B.A., DeBacker, T.K., Ravindran, B., & Krows, A.J. (1999). Goals, values, and beliefs as predictors of achievement and effort in high school mathematics classes. *Sex Roles, 40*(5/6), 421–458. Retrieved from ProQuest database.

Kornuta, H. (2001). Teacher portfolios in the supervision process: A journey of discovery. *Dissertation Abstracts International, 62*(03). (UMI No. 3007292)

Lunenburg, F.C., & Irby, B.J. (2014). *Writing a successful thesis or dissertation: Tips and strategies for students in the social and behavioral sciences.* Thousand Oaks, CA: Corwin Press.

McGowan, G. (2003). *Use of communication technologies to improve interpersonal relationships of emotionally disturbed students.* Unpublished manuscript, School of Education, National University, La Jolla, CA.

Merriam, S. & Tisdell, E. (2016). *Qualitative research: A guide to design and implementation* (4th ed.). San Francisco: Josey-Bass.

Mertens, D. (2015). *Research methods in education and psychology* (4th ed.). Thousand Oaks, CA: Sage Publications.

Mruk, C. (2013). *Self-esteem and positive psychology: Research, theory, and practice* (3rd ed.). New York: Springer Publishing Company.

Noll, J.W. (Ed.). (2011). *Taking sides: Clashing views on controversial issues* (16th ed.). New York: McGraw-Hill.

Patton, M.Q. (2015). *Qualitative evaluation and research methods* (4th ed.). Newbury Park, CA: SAGE.

Paul, R. & Elder, L. (2007). *Critical thinking concepts and tools*. Dillon Beach, CA: Foundation for Critical Thinking Press.

Piaget, J. (1954). *The construction of reality in the child* (M. Cook, Trans.). New York: Basic. Books.

Pyrczak, F., & Bruce, R.R. (2000). *Writing empirical research reports* (3rd ed.). Los Angeles, CA: Pyrczak Publishing.

Springer, K. (2010). *Educational research: A contextual approach*. Hoboken, NJ: John Wiley & Sons, Inc.

Trochim, W., & Donnelly, J. (2007). *The research methods knowledge base (3rd ed.). Mason, OH: Thomson*.

VanSolkema, L. (2003). *The formation of math confidence: A study of perceptions and experiences of high school girls*. Unpublished master's thesis, National University, La Jolla, CA.

Appendix A

Rubric for evaluating writing

We have found the rubric below to be very helpful in at least three ways:

1. When shared with students prior to their writing, it communicates criteria upon which their writing will be evaluated, and thereby supports their learning in the process of writing.
2. It provides instructors with criteria upon which to judge and report students' learning.
3. Over time, rubric scores provide evidence of overall student achievement, and achievement in relation to specific outcomes that can inform curricular change.

We have also found that students' writing has been further enhanced by providing them with completed examples of exemplary writing of the kind they are required to complete.

Table A.1
Rubric for evaluating writing

Level of achievement / Category*	Outstanding Value =	Commendable Value =	Growth area Value =	Assessment
Clarity, accuracy, and precision (APA, 2010, pp. 61, 65–70)	• Meaning is consistently clear and has no ambiguity. Relevant examples clearly illustrate ideas. • All ideas are expressed precisely, smoothly and with economy of expression (APA, 2010, p. 65). • Supporting evidence is consistently present. • Relevant detail is consistently used to clarify meaning.	• Meaning is clear and has little ambiguity. Relevant examples illustrate most ideas. • Most ideas are expressed with precision, smoothness, and economy of expression. • Supporting evidence is usually present. • Relevant detail is usually used to help clarify	• Meaning is sometimes unclear and/ or has some ambiguity. • Some ideas require greater precision and clarity to enhance overall meaning. • Supporting evidence is often missing. • In places, additional detail is needed to	/

Relevance (APA, 2010, pp. 27–28)	• The information is relevant (clearly and consistently linked to the topic and purpose statement). • Convincing argument is made that the topic is important to P-12 students' learning.	• Most information presented is relevant (clearly linked to the topic and purpose statement). • Argument is made that the topic is important to P-12 students' learning.	• Some information presented is relevant (links between information and topic and purpose statement are missing). • Unclear argument or assumption is made that the topic is important to P-12 students' learning.	/
Depth and breadth (APA, 2010, pp. 10, 27–28)	• Significant issues directly related to the topic are addressed in detail.	• Most significant issues directly related to the topic are addressed in detail.	• Some issues are addressed well while others need greater detail.	/

(Continued)

Table A.1 *Continued*

Category* / Level of achievement	Outstanding Value =	Commendable Value =	Growth area Value =	Assessment
	• Clearly addresses alternate points of view on the topic or multiple perspectives. • All claims are based on authoritative sources. • Provides compelling evidence of what works and why a strategy is effective.	• Addresses alternate points of view on the topic or includes more than one perspective. • Most claims are based on authoritative sources. • Provides evidence of what works and why a strategy is effective.	• Limited presentation of alternate points of view. • Additional authoritative sources are needed to support claims. • Provides limited evidence of what works and why a strategy is effective.	

| **Logic** (APA, 2010, pp. 61–64) | • Headings provide evidence of a clear, detailed outline, and well-ordered flow of thought.

• Ideas are consistently sequenced in an orderly way.

• Citations clearly and consistently support the logic of argument and purpose statement. | • Headings provide evidence of an outline and flow of thought.

• Most ideas are sequenced in an orderly way.

• Citations support the logic of argument and purpose statement. | • Some changes in headings or additional headings or paragraphs would clarify flow of thought.

• Some ideas are sequenced in an orderly way.

• Citations sometimes support the logic of argument and purpose statement. | / |
| **Mechanics of English** (APA, 2010, pp. 67–70, 77–86 & Chapter 4) | • Spelling and grammar are error free. | • Spelling and grammar are mostly error free. | • Spelling and grammatical errors are sometimes distracting. | / |

(Continued)

Table A.1 *Continued*

Level of achievement / *Category**	*Outstanding Value =*	*Commendable Value =*	*Growth area Value =*	*Assessment*
	• Sentence and paragraph construction consistently contribute to understanding. • Expression of thought is not obscured by mechanics.	• Sentence and paragraph construction contribute to understanding. • Expression of thought is rarely obscured by mechanics.	• Sentence and/or paragraph structure is occasionally awkward. • Expression of thought is sometimes obscured by mechanics.	
APA formatting, abstract, Table of Contents	• All sources are accurately cited in the body and reference section using current APA style (APA, 2010, pp. 169, 174–192).	• Most sources are accurately cited in the body and reference section using current APA style (APA, 2010, pp. 169,	• Few or no sources are accurately cited in the body and reference section using current APA style (APA, 2010, pp. 169,	/

	• Headings follow APA format (APA, 2010, p. 62).	• Most headings follow APA format (APA, 2010, p. 62).	• Few or no headings follow APA format (APA, 2010, p. 62).
	• Abstract is accurate, self-contained, concise, and specific, nonevaluative (APA, 2010, pp. 25–27).	• Abstract is accurate (APA, 2010, pp. 25–27).	• Abstract is not accurate (APA, 2010, pp. 25–27).
	• Table of Contents is consistent with chapter headings and distinguishes levels appropriately.	• Table of Contents is consistent with chapter headings.	• Table of Contents is not consistent with chapter headings.
Other grading factors			/
Total /			/

*The categories, Clarity, accuracy, and precision through Logic, are from Paul & Elder (2007).

Appendix B

APA skill building exercises*

*For additional exercises in APA format, see APA (2010b).

Exercise # 1. APA (6th ed.) references and citations: Where are the errors?

To strengthen your knowledge and skills in APA format, find the errors in the following citations and make the corrections. The answer key follows.

Pryczak, F, & Bruce, R. (2014) *Writing empirical research reports*. (8th Ed.). Routledge. NY:NY.

Darling-Hammond, L., Wilhoit, G., & Pittenger, L. (2014). *Accountability for college and career readiness: Developing a new paradigm*. Education Policy Analysis Archives, 22(86). Retrieved from *http://dx.doi.org/10.14507/epaa. v22n86.2014.*

Donmoyer, R. (2000). Generalizability and the single-case study. In Gomm, R., Hammersley, M., and Foster, P. (eds.). *Case study method* (pp. 45–68). Thousand Oaks, CA: SAGE Publications.

Goleman, D., Boyatzis, R., & McKee, A. (2002). Primal leadership: Realizing the power of emotional intelligence. Boston, MA: Harvard Business Press.

Patton, Michael Q. (2015). *Qualitative evaluation and research methods* (4th ed.). Newbury Park, CA: SAGE.

Palmer, P.J. (1999). Evoking the spirit in public education. *Educational Leadership, 56(4),* p 6–11.

Correct the following within text citations.
In his article, Parker Palmer (1999) notes that "the spiritual is always present in public education" (p. 8)/

Patton (2015) in his book, *Qualitative evaluation and research methods,* cited Locke, Spirduso, and Silverman who said . . .

Exercise #1. Answer key.

Pryczak, F., & Bruce, R. (2014). *Writing empirical research reports* (8th ed.). New York, NY: Routledge.

Darling-Hammond, L., Wilhoit, G., & Pittenger, L. (2014). Accountability for college and career readiness: Developing a new paradigm. *Education Policy Analysis Archives, 22*(86). Retrieved from *http://dx.doi.org/10.14507/epaa.v22n86.2014.*

Donmoyer, R. (2000). Generalizability and the single-case study. In R. Gomm, M. Hammersley, & P. Foster (Eds.), *Case study method* (pp. 45–68). Thousand Oaks, CA: SAGE Publications.

Goleman, D., Boyatzis, R., & McKee, A. (2002). *Primal leadership: Realizing the power of emotional intelligence.* Boston, MA: Harvard Business Press.

Patton, M.Q. (2015). *Qualitative evaluation and research methods* (4th ed.). Newbury Park, CA: SAGE Publications.

Palmer, P.J. (1999). Evoking the spirit in public education. *Educational Leadership, 56*(4), 6–11.

Within text citations.

Palmer (1999) noted that, "The spiritual is always present in public education" (p. 8).

Patton (2015) cited Locke, Spirduso, and Silverman who said . . .

[Note: If Locke, Spirduso, and Silverman have been previously cited in the writing, then the sentence would read: Patten (2015) cited Locke et al. who said . . .]

Exercise #2. APA (6th ed.) Writing style and citations

Strengthen your knowledge and skills in APA formatting by completing the following exercises. The answer key follows.

1. Why is it important to present different perspectives when presenting information on controversial issues?
2. Rewrite the following sentence for improved flow and clarity:

   We conducted an open-ended survey with the participants. This was done to learn their perceptions of the issue.
3. Rewrite the following sentence so that it is gender neutral: The research showed that a student scored higher on the test if he was involved in extra-curricular activities.
4. Edit the following citations:

   a. Gay, Mills, & Airasian, 2015, defined reliability as the degree to which a test or instrument consistently gives the same measure.

b. Correlational research investigates the relationship between variables and whether the relationship is positive or negative. Correlational research does not usually establish a cause and effect relationship (Gay et al., 2012; Trochim and Donnelly, 2007; Ary et al., 2006).

c. "The tendency for subjects to change their behavior just because of the attention gained from participating in an experiment has been referred to as the Hawthorne effect" (Ary et. al, 2006, page 301).

d. In their book, Understanding Research, Vicki Clark and John Creswell (2010) cite the Carrington, Templeton, and Papinczak (2003) study of the perceptions of friendship faced by teenagers diagnosed with Asperger syndrome.

Exercise #2. Answer key.

1. Presenting different perspectives adds to the scholarly review of issues surrounding the topic. It helps to avoid the appearance of bias. Review the information about contrasting views and differing perspectives on pages 11, 14, 33 and 42 of this text. Also, information on bias is found on pages 24, 25, and 26.

2. The researcher conducted an open-ended survey with the participants to determine their perceptions of the issue. Avoid the use of pronouns such as "we" and "this", as it may leave the meaning unclear.

3. The research showed that a student scored higher on the test if s/he was involved in extra-curricular activities.
   Or: The research showed that students scored higher on the test if they were involved in extra-curricular activities.

4. Edited citations:

   a. Gay, Mills, and Airasian (2015) defined reliability as the degree to which a test or instrument consistently gives the same measure. [Note: Use "&" within brackets and in the reference section; otherwise use "and".]

b. Correlational research investigates the relationship between variables and whether the relationship is positive or negative. Correlational research does not usually establish a cause and effect relationship (Ary et al., 2006; Gay et al., 2012; Trochim & Donnelly, 2007). [Note: Multiple authors are arranged alphabetically as in the reference section, rather than ordered by date of publication.]

c. "The tendency for subjects to change their behavior just because of the attention gained from participating in an experiment has been referred to as the Hawthorne effect" (Ary et al., 2006, p. 301). [Note: The period after "al" in et al.; page is abbreviated as p.; multiple pages would show pp.]

d. Clark and Creswell (2010) cite the study by Carrington, Templeton, and Papinczak about the perceptions of friendship faced by teenagers diagnosed with Asperger syndrome. [Note: Avoid adding book titles within text. Titles belong in the reference section. List only the dates of the works you read, not the dates of sources cited by authors you read.]

Appendix C

Examples of purpose statements

The following are examples of purpose statements used in Action Research.

> *The purpose of this quantitative Action Research study is to determine the relationship between a program, Science Process Skills, and a measure of science process skill improvement in grade eight science students, at . . . .*

It should be noted that the preceding statement could be quite different depending on the researcher's time, resources, and overarching purpose. For example, to strengthen the reliability of the findings, it would be helpful to have one or more control groups of students who were taught the same science concepts, but not with the particular Science Process Skills program. Greater time and effort would be needed to carry out such a study. However if the researcher's purpose is to get a window into whether the Science Process Skills program is making a difference in students' learning, s/he might compare measures of students' learning from a group who completed the program in the current year, and a similar group of students who completed similar concepts and the same test at an earlier (or later) time.

The same research topic from a qualitative perspective might be written as follows: *The purpose of this study is to discover the strengths and limitations of the Science Process Skills program from the perceptions of tenth grade science teachers.* Such a study might be carried out by interviewing teachers and/or designing and carrying out a survey that might include both open ended and closed responses.

The purpose of this research study is to determine the relationship between a measure of teacher experience and measures of student achievement within . . . School District. Teachers who had taught for a three-year period or more were identified as experienced teachers. Class results on Achievement Tests were compared to teacher experience to determine if a statistically significant relationship existed between teacher experience and this measurement of student achievement.

The purpose of this qualitative study is to discover the specific needs of adolescent students with developmental disabilities who experience comorbidity with social skills deficit or depression. It is hoped that the findings of the study will provide some insight to special educators and counselors for the creation of a school program that promotes emotional well-being, effective instruction, and safe learning for the special emotional needs of students with learning and developmental differences.

The purpose of this study is to discover, from the perceptions and experiences of parents at . . . School, what types of school involvement are most beneficial, what influences parent involvement, and what the role of various stakeholders should be to increase parental involvement. The questions used to interview parents are derived from the purpose statement.

Appendix D

Research planning organizer

The following organizer can be used to guide your thinking as well as to plan Chapters One, Two, and Three of your research study. There is also equivalent information in the chapter sections of this Guide.

Chapter One: Getting started

Chapter One purpose.

The purpose of Chapter One is to set the stage for your study and present an overview of the whole study. Your purpose statement must be a clear, precise statement that encapsulates what you intend to do in your study. The purpose statement provides a guide for everything you write in your study. Each time you repeat your purpose statement in your study, be sure it is a copy and paste of the statement approved by your instructor.

Complete a response to sections A, B, C, D, and E below.

A. Your interest.

What general topic related to your practice are you interested in investigating?

It is important to choose a topic about which you feel passionate; however, one caution is in order. You must not begin your study with the intent to 'prove' something. Like a good detective, you must gather information and look for evidence with an open mind. Accurate analysis of reliable data will allow you to speak authoritatively after you carry out your study. Wherever possible, it is important to provide differing and/or opposing perspectives on the issues that are at the heart of your topic.

B. Problem.

In regard to the topic you identified, what is the current situation? What is the problem, need, or issue that you would like to address?

The first step to solving a problem is to define it as clearly and precisely as possible. A clearly defined problem will make it much easier to write a laser sharp purpose statement that will guide your study.

Describe a problem you would like to explore and then formulate a question. The information you write in this section can be used in Chapter One of your study.

C. Background.

What has led up to your choosing your particular study?

After you have written the Literature Review (Chapter Two) you may add to responses to the preceding questions by *briefly* summarizing the main points (in one or two paragraphs). The information you write in this section can be used in Chapter One of your study.

D. Significance of the study.

Who will benefit from the results of your study? Why would it be important to carry out the study? What will happen if nothing is done?

For example, if your topic was about investigating whether use of a specific reading program raised students' reading scores, the results of your study would be of significance to your own students because reading is so vital to learning. Such a study would also have significance for parents, educators, and researchers.

The information you write in this section can be used in Chapter One of your study.

E. What will you measure (or who would you interview or survey) to gather data?.

For example, measures of whether an intervention is successful could come from such things as test scores, office referrals, attendance, et cetera. Such numerical data is called *quantitative* data. Or you could discover what you need to learn by interviewing people who have experienced what you are investigating. Such verbal or written data is called *qualitative* data.

While each study is unique, the information in A through E (above) will be relevant to your writing of Chapter One and the purpose statement will guide the whole of your study.

While it is important for you to think through each of the items above and include the information in Chapter One, you will begin by writing the Literature Review, Chapter Two.

Chapter One is an introductory chapter that provides a general overview of your study. An outline for Chapter One should be evident in the headings you use throughout the chapter. Review the example papers in the Resources section of the course website to see how headings and citations should appear in Chapter One.

Use the information below in conjunction with planning to write the Literature Review (Chapter Two) and preparing your methodology (Chapter Three).

Chapter Two: Begin the writing of your study with the Literature Review

Chapter Two purpose.

Chapter Two sets the theoretical basis for your study.

- Be sure to read this Guide, Chapter Two.
- Chapter Two reports what others have written about the topic, and reports about the methodology and findings of studies that relate to your topic.
- It is important to report opposing views and differing perspectives on the topic.
- It is important to organize a very clear outline for Chapter Two and make the outline visible to the reader through the use of headings.

Time commitment to Chapter Two.

It is important to being writing Chapter Two as soon in the course as possible. Chapter Two is by far, the most time-consuming chapter to write. By comparison, Chapters One and Three will take much less time to complete.

Beginning and organizing Chapter Two.

Use a graphic organizer (samples can be found in this Guide) to map your ideas around topic areas and to plan the organization of your chapter.

Begin Chapter Two by (re)stating the purpose of your study and restating the purpose (copy and paste your purpose statement each time you use it) and identify what is to come in Chapter Two by listing the main points of the outline of the chapter.

The main points will be summarized by a title that you will use as a heading, usually followed by sub-headings. These headings are required to follow an APA (2010b, p. 65) format as described below:

Table D.1
Format for APA levels of headings

Format for five levels of headings	
Level of heading	*Format*
1	**Centered, Boldface, Uppercase and Lowercase Heading**
2	**Flush Left, Boldface, Uppercase and Lowercase Heading**
3	**Indented, boldface, lowercase paragraph heading ending with a period.**
4	***Indented, boldface, italicized, lowercase paragraph heading ending with a period.***
5	*Indented, italicized, lowercase paragraph heading ending with a period.*

Format for Chapter Two.
The format for your Chapter Two will look like the following:

Chapter Two: Literature Review.
Introduction . . . in which you state the purpose of your study clearly and precisely and state what is to come in Chapter Two by listing the main points of the outline of the chapter. For example, you might write: "the purpose of this study is to . . . In Chapter Two a review of literature includes . . ." then list the main headings in the chapter. The headings will reflect what you have found to be important elements to report about the topic you have chosen. Remember that you cannot write exhaustively about your topic. Doing so would

require a book. Your purpose statement should serve as a guide for what you address in your Literature Review.

Report relevant information from your reading of peer reviewed sources. The headings you use should reflect the order in which you listed the main parts of your Literature Review in the introduction.

Use of headings is expected in scholarly writing to guide readers through the logic of your presentation. While there is a specific APA Manual (APA, 2010b) format for headings (p. 62), there is not 'one best way' to organize or outline *your* Literature Review. Translate your outline into headings as a way to clearly show how your flow of thought is organized.

An important part of scholarly writing is citing and referencing sources of information. The difference between an outstanding scholarly report and plagiarism can be as little as citing (or failure to cite) the source of information and ideas. If in doubt about whether to cite a source, cite the source.

The APA Manual describes and illustrates how to accurately cite and reference the articles and books you use.

End Chapter Two with a brief summary of what you have written. No new information should be included in the summary.

In review, this section of the organizer is intended for you to identify the main points in your Chapter Two. Be sure to use your purpose statement to guide and organize your writing.

You may need to add to or change the points you list, depending on what you find as you read in preparation for writing your Literature Review.

Chapter Three: Methodology

Chapter Three purpose.
Chapter Three presents the methodology for your study based on the unique purpose statement of your study.

As with Chapters One and Two, headings should be used to reflect an outline and the flow of thought in your writing.

Beginning and organizing Chapter Three.
Your draft of Chapter Three should provide your plan for conducting your research.

Use the following headings to add details to your notes.

Research design.
  Type of methodology.
  Why methodology was chosen.

Site selection.
  Setting description.

Population identification.

Participants in the study.
  Selection procedures.

Measuring instruments.

Data collection.

Data analysis.

Institutional Research Board approval.

Appendix E

Guide for scholarly writing

Scholarly writing is different from other types of writing. The purpose of scholarly writing is to communicate clearly, precisely, with relevance, and with evident logic about a topic. Therefore, in your writing, say what you need to say in a clear, precise, relevant, and logical way, and then stop writing.

The five points listed below provide guidance for your scholarly writing.

1. Create an outline for what you will write

    a. The points in the outline should appear as headings within your writing
    b. The headings act as directional signs for readers
    c. The outline and headings communicate your flow of thought

2. Say what you are going to write about in an introductory paragraph

    a. Introduce your topic
    b. When possible, say something general about the topic and cite a source

        i. The general statement helps set the context for your topic

  ii. A citation communicates early to the reader that you are writing a scholarly article – not just opinion

3. Say what you need to say to accomplish the purpose of your writing

  a. Follow your outline, using headings (or if you create an outline after writing, be sure the outline and headings show a clear flow of thought)

  b. Avoid writing simply to add additional pages

  c. Cite, cite, cite your sources of information

    i. The difference between plagiarism and academic honesty is in giving credit for ideas and quotes from other writers

    ii. Citations should direct readers to the sources you actually read

    iii. Use APA format

4. Say what you said in a summary paragraph

  a. Use the main headings of your outline to briefly review what you wrote about

  b. No new information should appear in the summary

5. Provide references in APA format for the authors/works cited. Table E.1 provides direction about where to find various topics in the APA Manual (6th ed.).

Table E.1
Where to find it in the APA Manual

Topic: Where to find information about . . .	Page in APA Manual (6th ed.)
Abbreviations (for references list)	180
Abstract	25–27
And/& (when to use)	175

(Continued)

Table E.1 *Continued*

Topic: Where to find information about . . .	Page in APA Manual (6th ed.)
Appendixes and supplemental materials	38–40
Article or chapter in edited book (how to reference)	184
As cited in (when to use for secondary sources)	178
Audiovisual media (how to reference)	209–210
Book and chapter references	202–205
Colon and semicolon (when to use)	89–90
Ellipsis points (when to use)	172–173
Et al. (when to use)	175, 177
Figures (types and how to label)	151–161
Footnotes (types and when to use)	37–38
Headings: Levels	62–63
Internet sources (how to reference)	214–215
Itemized or sequenced steps (seriation: numbered lists or bulleted lists)	63–65
Journal article references	198–202
Levels of headings	62–63
Multiple authors (how to reference)	177, 184

Topic: Where to find information about . . .	Page in APA Manual (6th ed.)
Numbers (when to use them as numbers and words)	111–114
Order of references	181–183
Pagination, order of pages, running head	229–230
Personal communication	179
Punctuation (when to use/not use various punctuation)	87–96
Quotation marks (guidelines for when to use)	91–92
Quotation of more than 40 words	92, 171
Reasonable exceptions (great commonsense advice)	5, 7
Reference examples	193–224
References page	37, 180
Spacing	229
Tables (presentation and labeling)	125–150

Appendix F

Guide for oral presentations

The oral presentation is an opportunity for students to share their learning process and product. The presentation may be a requirement by the institution to advance the proposal to the research stage and as part of the defense of a thesis or dissertation. See your institution's specific instructions and consult with your committee chair.

The following information provides guidelines and helpful hints for the oral presentation of the research study:

- To advance the proposal to the research stage, Chapters One, Two, and Three are part of the oral presentation.
- As part of the defense of a thesis or dissertation, all chapters are part of the oral presentation. The proposal and research sections should each be approximately ten minutes in length. It may be helpful to have a partner to keep track of time.
- Use visual tools to assist with the presentation.
- Use the Abstract to provide an outline of your presentation.
- Introduce your presentation and provide a brief overview.
- Include highlights of the problem, purpose and significance, research question(s), Literature Review and its contribution to the purpose, choice of methodology, kind of population,

data collection instrumentation and procedures, summary of findings, conclusions, and recommendations for change and further study.
- Invite questions.

The outcome of the oral presentation will provide direction from your committee about any changes that may be needed. Overall, it is one of the final processes for the research study and a celebration of the learning journey.

Index